The Early American
SONGBOOK

The Early American SONGBOOK

Based on the Alan Landsburg television series *The American Idea*

Compiled and edited, with original arrangements,

by Lee Vinson

Foreword by Irving Lowens

Illustrations by Susan Swan

A Rutledge Book
Prentice-Hall, Inc.
Englewood Cliffs, N.J.

ISBN: 0-13-222778-9

Library of Congress Catalog Card Number: 74-76864

Copyright © 1974 by Alan Landsburg Productions, Inc.

Musical arrangements copyright © 1974 by Module Music
and The Ridge Press, Inc.–Rutledge Books Division

Prepared and produced by The Ridge Press, Inc.–Rutledge
Books Division, 25 West 43 Street, New York, N.Y. 10036

Published in 1974 by Prentice-Hall, Inc., Englewood Cliffs, N.J.

Printed in the United States of America

CONTENTS

PSALM-TUNES, HYMNS, AND SINGING-SCHOOL SONGS   125

FOREWORD

From the very beginning, this was a singing land.

We sometimes forget that it was the American wilderness that was wild, and not the Europeans who crossed the Atlantic Ocean in their little wind-blown ships. We sometimes forget that those who settled New England came from an old England where music was omnipresent. We sometimes forget that the first settlers were the inheritors of the golden age of Elizabethan culture.

It is true, of course, that space was precious on board those crowded little trans-Atlantic vessels, and only the essentials could be transported. Musical instruments were not among the essentials—one could make do very well in the wilderness without a harpsichord or even a lute. But human voices and memories took up no room, and the family Bible and psalmbook were essentials; and since the regular singing of the psalms was one of the ordinances of the Pilgrim and Puritan sects, song was important in seventeenth-century New England life. As Governor Winthrop said about the Pilgrims when they set sail from Leyden for the New World, many of the congregation "were very expert in music."

But life was hard in the wilderness, and there was little time for amenities. The sons and daughters of the first settlers did not grow up in Elizabethan England, and expertise in music in New England was no help when it came to protecting their communities from the assaults of the Indians and the weather. To them, firing a flintlock accurately and wielding an axe skillfully were much more important activities than the ability to sing a complex Ainsworth Psalter tune accurately and sweetly. It was hardly surprising that the ability to read musical notation gradually became a lost art. By the beginning of the eighteenth century, the quality of New England singing had deteriorated to the point where it offended the sensibilities of the intelligentsia, and the repertory of tunes necessary to sing through the Book of Psalms had shrunk to an almost irreducible minimum.

Some sort of reform was plainly called for, and spearheaded by three bright young Harvard graduates—the Reverends Thomas Symmes, John Tufts, and Thomas Walter—it transpired around 1720. These men and their associates called for an end to the chaos that characterized congregational singing by advocating the establishment of "singing schools," where citizens could be taught the rudiments of music, and, having learned how to read musical notation, could quickly master new tunes. At first, the singing-school movement engendered bitter hostility, especially from diehards who insisted that what was good enough for their fathers was good enough for them. For them, music was an oral tradition, something passed down from generation to generation by word of mouth, and the "new way" of reading music from books was a revolutionary concept. But gradually reason prevailed, and even though minor skirmishes in the "Singing School War" were still taking place after the Revolution, the battle had really been won long before. By the 1760s, when Americans were beginning to chafe under the restrictions imposed upon them by the Mother Country, the singing school as a social institution was firmly established.

Originally, the demand for new tunes occasioned by the growing number of singing schools was supplied by England, and the names of such obscure tunesmiths as William Tans'ur, Joseph Stephenson, and Aaron Williams became well known in the colonies. But as trade decreased, Americans took up the slack. Our musical Declaration of Independence took place in 1770, when William Billings, a Boston singing master, issued *The New-England Psalm-Singer,* the first published collection of singing school music entirely composed by an American. By the 1780s, the trickle of American tune books had become a sizable stream, and by the 1790s the stream had become a flood. Thousands of tunes composed by Americans were in print; the singing school had brought about the first great flowering of American musical creativity.

For all this there is ample documentary and testamentary evidence; to establish the existence of folk and secular singing traditions is somewhat more difficult, however. We can infer that such traditions did, in fact, exist in the seventeenth century from condemnatory references to folk songs and ballads in sermons by fire-eating clergymen, as well as from the few extant examples of words and music copied into the commonplace books of Harvard students. And then as now, there were popular songs of the day, some of them old favorites, some of them the hit tunes of English musical shows, which were performed with increasing frequency in the colonies beginning in the 1730s. But aside from singing school music, all printed music was imported from the Old Country. Music publishing as an American industry was late in starting—it did not really begin to flourish until the 1790s.

In light of this state of affairs, it is not terribly surprising that (at least until the music-publishing industry was firmly established) the number of truly popular songs on this side of the Atlantic was counted in the dozens rather than the hundreds. This fact led to a curious result, seemingly unique to this country—the parody became the most popular form of American vocal expression. Our newspapers were full of topical verses written in the metrical patterns of the favorite songs of the day. Sometimes the poet would help out the reader by making a reference to the tune to which the words were to be sung ("Tune, 'Down Derry Down'" or "To be sung to the tune of 'Yankee Doodle'" were typical instances). But not infrequently the pattern was so distinctive (as in such tunes as "God Save the King" or "To Anacreon in Heaven") that such references could be safely omitted with no danger of confusion. In large part, the parodies of the period were patriotic or political in subject matter. And they were ephemeral, songs of the moment to be supplanted in a day or a week by another set of words for the same tune. The most lasting were anthologized and published in book or pamphlet format conveniently designed to be carried in pocket or purse; these so-called songsters were omnipresent on the American scene in the second half of the eighteenth century.

What about *real* composers in the European sense? Were there no minor Handels or Haydns on the American scene? There were a few. Represented in this anthology are Francis Hopkinson, man of many talents, and the professional musicians (and immigrants all) James Hewitt, Alexander Reinagle, Peter Von Hagen, George K. Jackson, and Benjamin Carr, honorable men and pioneers. But they were distinctly minor figures, and they occupy a distinctly minor place in the broader picture of early American song. This was a singing land, but very few of our forefathers busied themselves singing the songs of our serious composers. They were too busy singing Billings's rousing "Chester" at some patriotic gathering, or Timothy Swan's strange "China" at a funeral, or bawling out the latest set of words to "Heart of Oak."

The excellent collection of early American songs you hold in your hands can do no more than hint at the wealth of material that is available. May it inspire further and deeper voyages of discovery into the American musical heritage, as yet still largely *terra incognita.*

Irving Lowens

PREFACE

Early American composers were often self-taught musicians and were not always familiar with the rules of traditional harmony. In making the musical arrangements of their songs, I found it necessary in some cases to revise their harmonizations. Altering chord choices and bass lines was inevitable when correcting such anachronisms as parallel fifths, parallel octaves, and doubled leading tones. In cases where the original melodies were pitched too high for the untrained voice, I have transposed them to a lower pitch to accommodate the range of the average singer. In part writing the tenor voice usually carried the melody; here it has been interchanged with the soprano.

Compiling a music book such as this requires the aid of a variety of people, including historians, musicologists, librarians, collectors, editors, and typographers. The quality of the finished product is largely a reflection of their competent assistance. Out of all these people four names come to mind, without whose guidance and encouragement this book could not have been completed: Irving Lowens, historian of early American music and music critic for the *Washington Star-News*; Richard Jackson, Head of the Americana Collection, Music Division, New York Public Library; Maud Cole, of the Rare Book Division, New York Public Library; and Mimi Koren, editor at Rutledge Books.

LEE VINSON

I
Patriotic
Songs

One Penny Sheet

In Congress, July 4, 1776.

A DECLARATION
By the Representatives of the
UNITED STATES OF AMERICA,
In General Congress Assembled.

HOW STANDS
THE GLASS AROUND?

An early version of this song, also known as "Why, Soldiers, Why?"
was originally published in 1710 in London for use by a small
theater in Haymarket. The British general James Wolfe is said to
have sung it at a meeting of his officers, on the eve of the resounding
British victory over the French at Quebec in September, 1759—
hence it has acquired another name, "Wolfe's Song."

Although the story of Wolfe's singing it may be a myth, the song
nevertheless was a favorite among American colonial soldiers.

Moderately

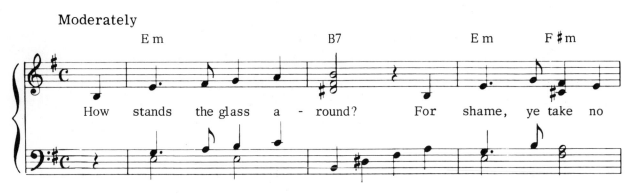

How stands the glass a - round? For shame, ye take no

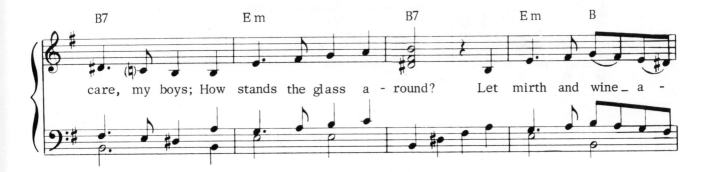

care, my boys; How stands the glass a - round? Let mirth and wine _ a -

bound. The trum - pets _ sound! The col - ors fly - ing _

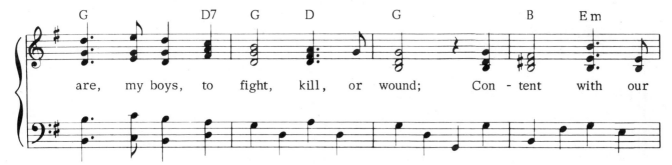

are, my boys, to fight, kill, or wound; Con - tent with our

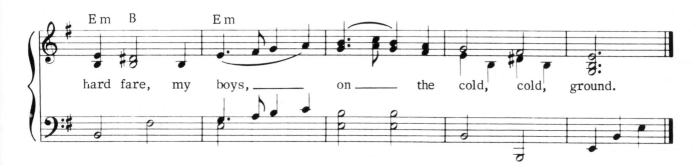

hard fare, my boys, _____ on _____ the cold, cold, ground.

Why, soldiers, why?
Should we be melancholy, boys?
Why, soldiers, why?
Whose bus'ness 'tis to die!
What? Sighing? Fie!
Drink on, drown fear, be jolly, boys,
'Tis he, you, or I.
Cold, hot, wet, or dry
We're always bound to follow, boys,
And scorn to fly.

'Tis but vain
(I mean not to upbraid you, boys),
'Tis but vain
For soldiers to complain.
Should next campaign
Send us to Him that made you, boys,
We're free from pain;
But should we remain,
A bottle and a kind landlady
Cures all again.

15

BRAVE WOLFE

This lovely ballad is one of several that appeared after the capture of Quebec by the British in 1759. It was inspired by the news that General James Wolfe, the British commander at the battle, had widowed one of the more beautiful women in England when he "expired in the arms of victory." The Dorian mode of the melody, written by an unknown composer, and the quaint language of the text effectively capture much of the refined quality of the eighteenth century. The text was first published in Boston in 1759.

Moderately slow

"Come, all you young men_ all, let_ noth-ing_ fright you, Nor

your ob-jec-tion_ make, nor_ let it de-light you; Let

not your cour-age_ fail till_ af-ter the trial, Let

16

not your fan - cy___ move   at   the first de - ni - al."

"I sat down by my love thinking to enjoy her,
"I took her by the hand not to delude her;
"When I attempt to speak, my tongue doth quiver,
"I dare not speak my mind whilst I am with her."

"Here is a chain of gold, long time I've kept it,
"Here is a ring of gold, madam, if you'll accept it;
"When you this posy read, think on the giver,
"Madam, remember me or I'm undone forever."

Then this brave youth took to the ocean,
To free America of those invasions;
He landed at Quebec with all his party
That city to attack, being brave and hearty.

Wolfe drew up his men in a line so pretty,
On the plains of Abraham, before the city;
A distance from the town the French did meet him,
With a double number they resolved to beat him.

The French drew up their men, for death prepared,
In one another's face they stood and stared;
Whilst Wolfe and Montcalm together walked
Betwixt their armies they, like brothers, talked.

Then each man took his place at their retire,
And then this numerous host began their fire;
Suddenly from his horse fell this brave hero,
You may lament his loss in the wields of sorrow.

The French began to break their ranks and flying,
Wolfe seemed to revive whilst he lay a-dying;
He raised up his head where cannons rattle,
And to his army said: "How goes the battle?"

His aide-de-camp replied: "'Tis in our favor,
"Quebec and all her pride, nothing can save her;
"She falls into our hands with all her treasure."
"O, then," replied brave Wolfe, "I die with pleasure!"

Bad news is come to town, bad news is carried,
Some say her love is dead, some say he's married;
Bad news is come to town, she fell a-weeping,
They stole away her love while she was sleeping.

17

DEATH OF GENERAL WOLFE

The words of this once-popular song were written by Thomas Paine and were set to music by an unknown composer. The song was first published in the Pennsylvania Magazine of American Monthly Museum *for March, 1775, accompanied by the following note, presumably written by Paine: "Most of our heroes, both ancient and modern, are celebrated in song of some kind or other. . . . [In] tribute to our immortal Wolfe, I herewith send you one. I have not pursued the worn-out craft of modern song, but have thrown it into fable."*

In a mold - er - ing cave where the wretch - ed re-treat, Brit-

tan - ni - a sat wast - ed with care; She

wept for her Wolfe, then ex - claimed_ a - gainst fate, And

The sire of the gods from his crystal-
   line throne
Beheld the disconsolate dame,
And moved at her tears he sent Mer-
   cury down,
And these were the tidings that came:

Britannia forbear, not a sigh, not a
   tear,
For thy Wolfe so deservedly loved;
Your grief shall be changed into
   triumphs of joy,
For Wolfe is not dead but removed.

LIBERTY SONG

On July 18, 1768, "The Liberty Song" was published in the Boston Gazette. The words were written by John Dickinson, later a member of the First Continental Congress and also an officer in the Continental Army. One of our first patriotic songs, it subsequently appeared in various New England newspapers, where it became quite popular. Late in September of the same year, the text was distributed on a broadside, to be sung to the tune "Heart of Oak," an English air composed by Dr. William Boyce.

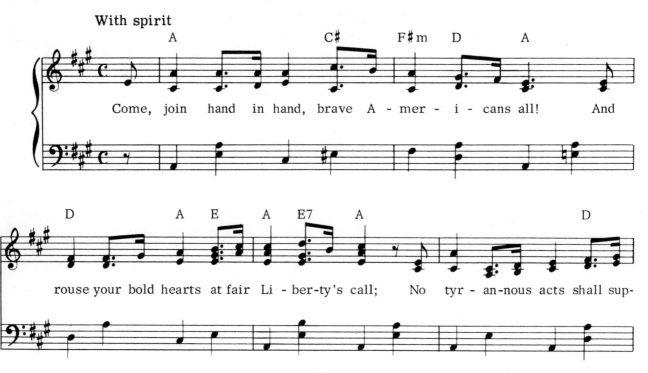

press your just claim, Or stain with dis-hon - or A - mer - i - ca's name.

Chorus:

In free-dom we're born, and in free-dom we'll live! Our purs-es are read-y,

Stead-y, friends, stead-y; Not as slaves,_ but as free men, our mon-ey we'll give.

Our worthy forefathers—let's give them a cheer!
To climates unknown did courage-ously steer;
Through oceans to deserts, for free-dom they came,
And, dying, bequeathed us their free-dom and fame.
Chorus:

Their generous bosoms all dangers despised,
So highly, so wisely, their birthrights they prized;
We'll keep what they gave, we will piously keep,
Nor frustrate their toils on the land or the deep.
Chorus:

How sweet are the labors that free-men endure,
That they shall enjoy all the profit, secure,

No more such sweet labors Americans know,
If Britons shall reap what Americans sow.
Chorus:

Then join hand in hand brave Ameri-cans all,
By uniting we stand, by dividing we fall;
In so righteous a cause let us hope to succeed,
For heaven approves of each generous deed.
Chorus:

This bumper I crown for our sover-eign's health,
And this for Britannia's glory and wealth;
That wealth and that glory immortal may be,
If she is but just, and we are but free.
Chorus:

COME, SHAKE YOUR
DULL NODDLES

Two months after "The Liberty Song" was published, the Boston
Gazette *printed this answer to it. The chorus more than any other
part of the parody indicates the general animosity existing between
the two sides:*

> In folly you're born, and in folly you'll live!
> To madness still ready, and stupidly steady;
> Not as men, but as monkeys, the tokens you give.

*The text—meant, like "The Liberty Song," to be sung to "Heart of
Oak"—was accompanied by a brief note: "Last Tuesday the following song made its appearance from a garret at Castle William." The
author is unknown.*

Come, shake your dull nod - dles, ye pump - kins, and bawl, And
own that you're mad at fair Li - ber - ty's call; No scan-dal-ous con - duct can

add to your shame, Con-demned to dis-hon - or, in - her - it the fame.

Chorus: In fol - ly you're born, and in fol - ly you'll live! To mad-ness still read-y, and stu-pid-ly stead-y; Not as men but as mon-keys, the to - kens you give.

Your grandsire, old Satan, now give
   him a cheer,
Would act like yourselves, and as
   wildly would steer;
So great an example in prospect still
   keep,
Whilst you are alive, Old Belza may
   sleep.
Chorus:

Such villains, such rascals, all dangers
   despise,
And stick not at mobbing when mis-
   chief's the prize;
They burst through all barriers, and
   piously keep
Such chattels and goods the vile rascals can sweep.
Chorus:

Then plunder, my lads, for when red
   coats appear,
You'll melt like the locust when
   winter is near;

Gold vainly will glow, silver vainly
   will shine,
But, faith, you must skulk, you no
   more shall purloin.
Chorus:

Then nod your poor numskulls, ye
   pumpkins, and bawl,
The de'il take such rascals, fools,
   whoresons, and all;
Your cursed old trade of purloining
   must cease,
The dread and the curse of all order
   and peace.
Chorus:

Gulp down your last dram, for the
   gallows now groans,
And, over-depressed, her lost empire
   bemoans;
While we quite transported and
   happy shall be,
From mobs, knaves, and villains, pro-
   tected and free.
Chorus:

MASSACHUSETTS LIBERTY SONG

Before the outbreak of the actual conflict in 1775, the political battle was often fought in print—and in song as well. "Massachusetts Liberty Song" was written by Dr. Benjamin Church as a retort to "Come, Shake Your Dull Noddles." Here the colonists voice their defiance of the tyrants who would "encroach on our rights," but affirm their loyalty to the king, "still firmly persuaded our rights he'll restore." The words and music were first published together in Bickerstaff's Boston Almanack for 1770.

Come, swal - low your bump - ers, ye Tor - ies, and roar, That the

sons of fair Free - dom are ham - pered once more; But know that no cut-throats our

spir - its can tame, Nor a host of op-pres-sors shall smoth - er the flame.

Chorus:

In free-dom we're born and, like sons of the brave, We'll nev - er sur-ren-der! But

swear to de-fend her, And scorn_ to sur-vive if un - ab - le to save.

Our grandsires, blest heroes! We'll give them a tear,
Nor sully their honors by stooping to fear;
Through deaths and through dangers their trophies they won,
We dare be their rivals nor will be outdone.
Chorus:

Our wives and our babes, still pro-tected, shall know,
Those who dare to be free shall for-ever be so;
On these arms and these hearts they may safely rely,
For in freedom we'll live or like heroes we'll die.
Chorus:

Not the glitter of arms nor the dread of a fray,
Could make us submit to their chains for a day;
Withheld by affection, on Britons we call:
Prevent the fierce conflict which threatens your fall!
Chorus:

Then join hand in hand, brave Amer-icans all!
To be free is to live, to be slaves is to fall;
Has the land such a dastard, as scorns not a lord,
Who dreads not a fetter much more than a sword?
Chorus:

25

CASTLE ISLAND SONG

There was considerable unrest in Boston after British troops were stationed there. British attempts to suppress the populace resulted in the "Boston Massacre" of March 5, 1770, in which several citizens were killed. The troops were forthwith consigned to barracks on Castle Island, where the verses of the following song were written soon after the event. One broadside described the song as "much in vogue among the friends to arbitrary power." The ballad was sung to the English tune "Down Derry Down."

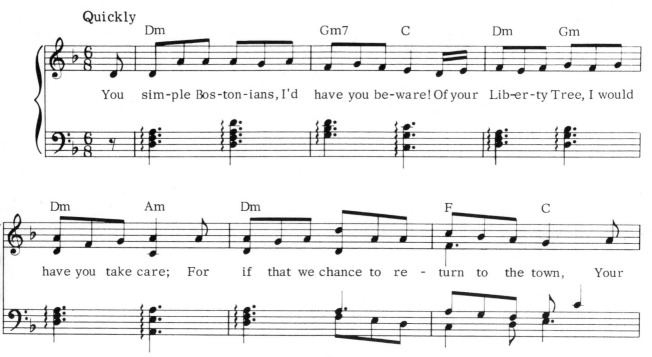

You sim-ple Bos-ton-ians, I'd have you be-ware! Of your Lib-er-ty Tree, I would have you take care; For if that we chance to re-turn to the town, Your

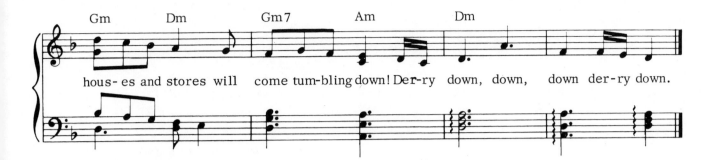

hous- es and stores will come tum-bling down! Der-ry down, down, down der-ry down.

If you will not agree to Old England's
laws,
I fear that King Hancock will soon
get the yaws;
But he need not fear, for I swear we
will,
For the want of a doctor give him a
hard pill.
    Derry down, down, down derry
    down.

A brave reinforcement, we soon think
to get,
Then we will make you poor pumpkins to sweat;
Our drums they'll rattle, and then
you will run
To the devil himself, from the sight
of a gun.
    Derry down, down, down derry
    down.

Our fleet and our army, they soon will
arrive,
Then to a bleak island, you shall not
us drive;
In every house you shall have three or
four,
And if that will not please you, you
shall have half a score.
    Derry down, down, down derry
    down.

FREE AMERICA

The words of this celebrated and spirited battle song, written by Dr. Joseph Warren, were first published in Massachusetts in 1770. Ironically, the text was intended to fit the melody of the patriotic English song "The British Grenadier." Dr. Warren, later killed at Bunker Hill, sent Paul Revere on his famous ride.

Moderately, marching

Lift up your hands, ye he - roes, And swear with proud dis - dain! The wretch that would en - snare you Shall lay his snares in vain. Should Eu - rope emp - ty all her force, We'll meet her in ar - ray; And

fight and shout, and shout and fight for__ North A - mer - i - ca!

Torn from a world of tyrants,
Beneath this western sky;
We formed a new dominion,
A land of liberty!
The world shall own we're masters
  here,
Then hasten on the day;
Huzza, huzza, huzza, huzza,
For free America!

THE BANKS OF THE DEE

The Dee river in Scotland provides a poetic setting for this lovely ballad, sung by a maiden lamenting the departure of her lover to "quell the proud rebels" in the colonies. The words were written by John Tait, a judge in one of the minor courts at Edinburgh, and were adapted to the traditional Irish air "Langolee." Tait wrote the song in 1775, "on the departure of a friend for America, to join the British Forces." It was popular both in England and in the colonies.

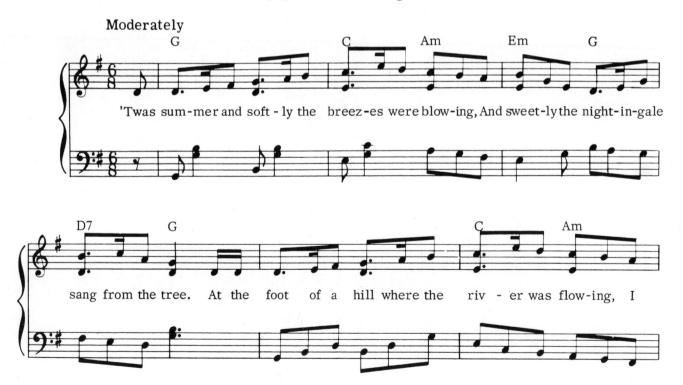

Moderately

'Twas sum-mer and soft - ly the breez-es were blow-ing, And sweet-ly the night-in-gale

sang from the tree. At the foot of a hill where the riv - er was flow-ing, I

sat my-self down on the banks of the Dee. Flow on, love-ly Dee, flow on, thou sweet riv-er; Thy banks, pur-est stream, shall be dear to me ev-er. For there I first gained the af-fec-tion and fa-vor of Ja-mie, the glo-ry and pride of the Dee.

But now he's gone from me and left me thus mourning,
To quell the proud rebels, for valiant is he;
But ah! there's no hope of his speedy returning,
To wander again on the banks of the Dee.
He's gone, hapless youth, o'er the rude roaring billows,
The kindest, the sweetest, of all his brave fellows,
And left me to stray 'mongst these once loved willows,
The loneliest lass on the banks of the Dee.

But time and my prayers may perhaps yet restore him,
Blest peace may restore my dear lover to me,
And when he returns, with such care I'll watch o'er him,
He never shall leave the sweet banks of the Dee.
The Dee then will flow, all its beauty displaying,
The lambs on its banks will again be seen playing,
Whilst I, with my Jamie, am care-lessly straying,
And tasting again all the sweets of the Dee.

31

A PARODY

This parody on "The Banks of the Dee" was written in 1775 by Oliver Arnold, a native of Connecticut and relative of the traitor Benedict Arnold. The song exhibits an excellent sense of humor as well as a refined skill in writing. Note especially the double meaning of the word "banks" suggested by the last two lines of the last verse:

And England thus honestly taxes defraying,
With natural drafts from the banks of the Dee.

banks of the Dee. Lead on, thou paid cap - tain! Tramp on, thou proud min - ions! Thy ranks, bas - est men, shall be strung like ripe on - ions; For here thou hast found heads with war - like o - pin-ions, On the shoul-ders of no - bles who ne'er saw the Dee.

Prepare for war's conflict, or make preparation
For peace with the rebels, for they're brave and glee;
Keep mindful of dying and leave the foul nation
That sends out its armies to brag and to flee.

Make haste, now, and leave us, thou miscreant Tories!
To Scotland repair! There court the sad houris,
And listen once more to their plaints and their stories
Concerning the "glory and pride of the Dee."

Be quiet and sober, secure and contented,
Upon your own land be valiant and free;
Bless God that the war is so nicely prevented,
And till the green fields on the banks of the Dee.

The Dee then will flow, all its beauty displaying,
The lambs on its banks will again be seen playing,
And England thus honestly taxes defraying,
With natural drafts from the banks of the Dee.

WHAT A COURT HATH OLD ENGLAND

Written in 1775, the lyrics of this song reflect the high level of tension that existed between the colonies and England prior to the actual fighting. Although the American cause was supported by such prominent Englishmen as the Earl of Chatham (William Pitt), Colonel Isaac Barré, Edmund Burke, and John Wilkes, armed conflict seemed inevitable, as illustrated by the last line, "And we'll die in defense of the rights of the land."

Set to the English tune "Down Derry Down," the text is a restatement of America's grievances and her willingness to right them by force if necessary.

What a court, hath old Eng-land, of fol-ly and sin; 'Spite of

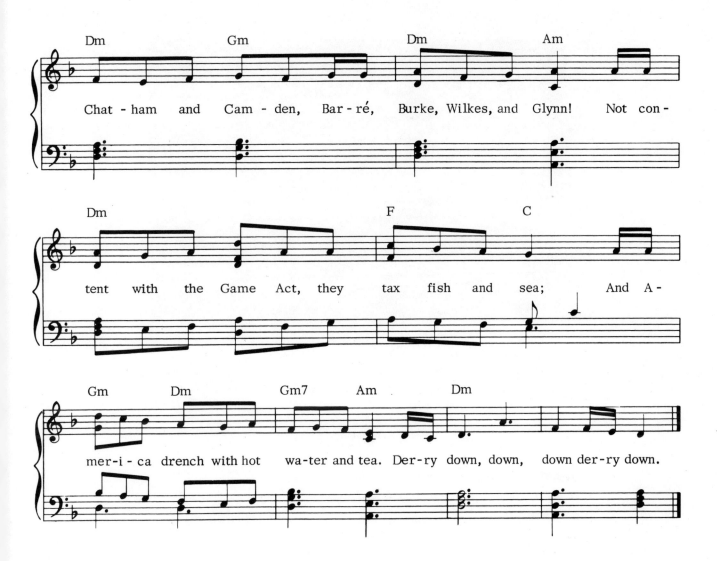

Chat - ham and Cam - den, Bar - ré, Burke, Wilkes, and Glynn! Not con-
tent with the Game Act, they tax fish and sea; And A-
mer-i - ca drench with hot wa-ter and tea. Der-ry down, down, down der-ry down.

There's no knowing where this oppression will stop;
Some say: "There's no cure but a
capital chop!"
And that I believe's each American's
wish,
Since you've drenched them with tea
and deprived them of fish.
    Derry down, down, down derry
    down.

Then freedom's the word, both at
home and abroad,
And out every scabbard that hides a
good sword!
Our forefathers gave us this freedom
in hand,
And we'll die in defense of the rights
of the land.
    Derry down, down, down derry
    down.

AMERICAN "HEART OF OAK"

J. W. Hewlings, the author of this ballad "on the present critical times," was a native of Virginia. The verses were published in 1775 and were intended to be sung to the melody "Heart of Oak." This was an English tune first composed in 1759, which was frequently used for both English and American songs—such as "The Liberty Song" and its parodies, above.

up for your right, And ne'er let our foes say we are put to the flight.

Chorus:

For so just is our cause and so val-iant our men; We al-ways are read-y,

Stead-y, boys, stead-y; We'll fight_ for our free-dom a-gain and a-gain.

The placemen and commoners have taken a bribe
To betray their own country and the empire beside;
And though the colonies stand condemned by some,
There are no rebels here, but are traitors at home.
Chorus:

The great Magna Charta is wounded severe,
By accounts from the doctors, 'tis almost past cure;
Let's defend it with the sword or die with the braves,
For we had better die in freedom than live and be slaves.
Chorus:

They tax us contrary to reason and right,
Expecting that we are not able to fight;
But to draw their troops home I do think would be best,
For Providence always defends the oppressed.
Chorus:

The valiant Bostonians have entered the field,
And declare they will fall there before they will yield;
A noble example! In them we'll confide,
We'll march to their town, stand or fall by their side.
Chorus:

THE AMERICAN HERO

The words of this stark war hymn were written by Nathaniel Niles (1741–1828). They are traditionally sung to a tune called "Bunker Hill," probably written by Andrew Law and published in Connecticut in 1781. The original setting was for four voices, with the melody in the tenor voice, as was customary at the time.

The Battle of Bunker Hill (June 17, 1775) made the colonials realize that they were at last definitely committed to a war against one of the leading military powers of the world. It was on Bunker Hill and nearby Breed's Hill outside Boston that over 1,500 American and British soldiers were killed or wounded, after the British charged three times uphill into an entrenched American army. The British lost over half their command. So strong was the memory of this battle that afterwards, whenever a British officer displayed initiative, it was said that he had not been at the battle of Bunker Hill.

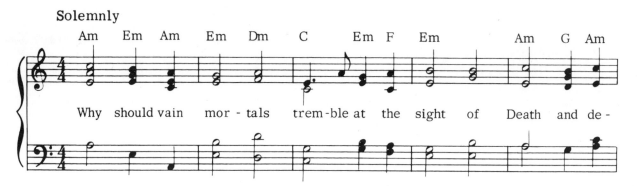

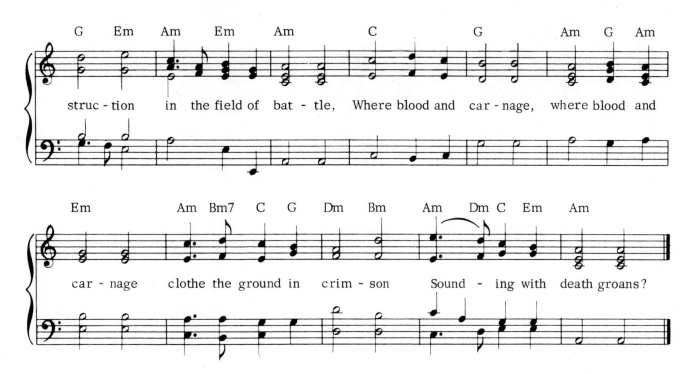

struc - tion in the field of bat - tle, Where blood and car - nage, where blood and

car - nage clothe the ground in crim - son Sound - ing with death groans?

Death will invade us by the means appointed,
And we must all bow to the king of terrors;
Nor am I anxious, nor am I anxious, if I am preparéd,
    What shape he comes in.

Good is Jehovah in bestowing sunshine,
Nor less his goodness in the storm and thunder;
Mercies and judgment, mercies and judgment, both proceed from kindness—
    Infinite kindness!

Then to the wisdom of my Lord and Master
I will commit all that I have or wish for;
Sweetly as babes sleep, sweetly as babes sleep will I give my life up
When called to yield it.

Now, Mars, I dare thee, clad in smoky pillars,
Bursting from bombshells, roaring from the cannon,
Rattling in grape shot, rattling in grapeshot like a storm of hailstones,
    Torturing Aether!

While all their hearts quick palpitate for havoc,
Let slip you bloodhounds, named the British Lions;
Dauntless as death stares, dauntless as death stares, nimble as the whirlwind,
    Dreadful as demons!

Let oceans waste on all your floating castles,
Fraught with destruction, horrible to nature;
Then, with your sails filled, then with your sails filled by a storm of vengeance,
    Bear down to battle!

Life, for my country and the cause of freedom,
Is but a trifle for a worm to part with;
And if preservéd, and if preservéd in so great a contest,
    Life is redoubled.

YANKEE DOODLE

The facts concerning the origin of "Yankee Doodle" are few, though the stories about it are many. The first verse, without music, appeared in the libretto of The Disappointment, a comic opera published in New York in 1767. The music, without words, was first published—as far as we know—in Scotland in 1782, and in America around 1794 as part of Benjamin Carr's "The Federal Overture." Authorities agree that the song is American in origin.

When Cornwallis surrendered at Yorktown in 1781, it is said that he did so to the fifing and drumming of the Continental Army playing this tune.

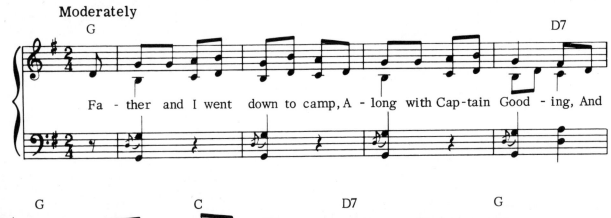

Chorus:

Yan - kee Doo - dle, keep it up, Yan - kee Doo - dle dan - dy,

Mind the mu - sic and the step, And with the girls be hand - y.

And there we saw a thousand men,
As rich as Squire David;
And what they wasted ev'ry day
I wish it could be savéd.
Chorus:

And there they had a swampin' gun
As large as a log of maple,
On a deuced little cart—
A load for father's cattle.
Chorus:

And every time they fired it off
It took a horn of powder;
It made a noise like father's gun,
Only a nation louder.
Chorus:

And there I saw a pumpkin shell
As big as mother's basin,
And every time they touched it off,
They scampered like the nation.
Chorus:

And there I saw a little keg,
Its heads were made of leather;
They knocked upon't with little sticks
To call the folks together.
Chorus:

And there was Captain Washington,
The gentlefolks about him;
They say he grows so 'ternal proud
He will not ride without them.
Chorus:

But I can't tell you half I saw,
They kept up such a smother;
So I took my hat off, made a bow,
And scampered home to mother.
Chorus:

CAPTURE OF BURGOYNE

This excellent Revolutionary War song was first published in Phila-delphia in 1842, "from a manuscript furnished the editor by John Ely, now in his eighty-fifth year, a soldier of the Revolution, who was at the capture of Burgoyne."

The capitulation of British General Burgoyne on October 17, 1777, at Saratoga greatly revived the colonial cause. Here an entire British army had been smashed, and the field had been won with honor and restraint.

Moderately fast

When Dis-cord did rear her black stand-ard on high, And sent her hoarse voice through the sky, the sky, Con-vuls-ing all na-ture with dread-ful a-larm; Then Free-dom com-mand-ed her he-roes from far, They

heard the proud sum-mons and shout-ed for war! Here you might see

youth of high spir - it, of gen - ius and mer - it, in arms.

O'er Champlain proud Burgoyne, all terrible, comes
With thundering cannon and drums, and drums,
He shook all the neighboring regions around;
Of blustering titles he told a long tale,
And thought pomp and nonsense would turn our cheek pale;
But then full soon bold Stark and his yeomen,
The glory of freemen, he found.

Three times in fierce combat the armies were joined,
But battle went not to his mind, his mind,
For American souls were too gallant to yield;
Amazed from the hill he beheld his hard fate,
And wished to retire when the hour was too late;
Sighing he saw his hundreds were dying,
His thousands were flying the field.

While hosts of brave patriots with hearts that beat high,
Rushed onward to conquer or die, or die,
Led by Gates, Morgan, Lincoln, those heirs of bright fame;
He saw skill and discipline ever must bend,
Where Freedom and Virtue and glory contend;
Humble and sad this haughty pretender
Was forced to surrender with shame.

Then the merry bells rang round American plains,
And pleasure enlivened the strains, the strains,
While Fame the bold acts of our warriors sung;
The breath of our heroes new ardor inspired,
New hopes the sad hearts of the timorous fired;
By Virtue's voice, like odors of even,
Sweet praise to high heaven was sung.

45

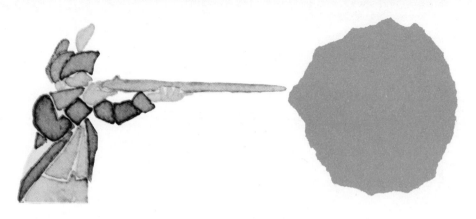

BATTLE OF THE KEGS

Early in 1778, the Americans set a number of "infernals" afloat in the Delaware River a few miles above Philadelphia, where several British ships were anchored. The infernals were kegs filled with gunpowder, designed to explode on contact. The city reacted with panic, and the British forces immediately manned all the wharves and the ships in the harbor. As a contemporary account relates (with tongue in cheek), "The battle began, and it was surprising to behold the incessant blaze that was kept up against the enemy, the kegs. Both officers and men exhibited the most unparalleled skill and bravery on the occasion . . . Lord Howe has despatched a swift-sailing packet, with an account of this victory, to the court at London. In a word, [this day] must ever be distinguished in history for the memorable battle of the kegs."

To commemorate the event, Francis Hopkinson, one of the signers of the Declaration of Independence, wrote this ballad. It is traditionally sung to the tune of "Yankee Doodle."

Chorus:

Yan - kee Doo - dle, keep it up, Yan - kee Doo - dle dan - dy,

Mind the mu - sic and the step, And with the girls be hand - y.

'Twas early day, as poets say,
Just when the sun was rising,
A soldier stood on a log of wood
And saw a thing surprising.
Chorus:

As in amaze he stood to gaze,
The truth can't be denied, sir,
He spied a score of kegs or more
Come floating down the tide, sir.
Chorus:

"These kegs, I'm told, the rebels bold,
"Packed up like pickled herring,
"And they're come down to attack the
    town
"In this new way of ferrying."
Chorus:

Now up and down throughout the
    town
Most frantic scenes were acted;
And some ran here and others there,
Like men almost distracted.
Chorus:

"Arise, arise!" Sir Erskine cries,
"The rebels—more's the pity,
"Without a boat, are all afloat,
"And ranged before the city."
Chorus:

"Therefore prepare for bloody war,
"These kegs must all be routed,
"Or surely we despised shall be,
"And British courage doubted."
Chorus:

The cannons roar from shore to shore,
The small arms make a rattle;
Since wars began, I'm sure no man
Ere saw so strange a battle.
Chorus:

The kegs, 'tis said, though strongly
    made
Of rebel staves and hoops, sir,
Could not oppose their powerful foes,
The conquering British troops, sir.
Chorus:

From morn till night, these men of
    might
Displayed amazing courage;
And when the sun was fairly down,
Retired to sup their porridge.
Chorus:

Such feats did they perform that day,
Against those wicked kegs, sir,
That years to come, if they get home,
They'll make their boasts and brags,
    sir.
Chorus:

A TOAST

The winter of 1777–1778 was the winter of suffering for George Washington's forces at Valley Forge. But in February, France signed a treaty of alliance with the newly proclaimed United States. Reassured by this event, and sustained by the courage of General Washington, Americans could now once more believe that victory would soon be theirs.

This modest drinking song was written by Francis Hopkinson in honor of the great leader, who was truly the "glory and pride" of the American people.

Moderately fast, spirited

'Tis Wash-ing-ton's health, fill a bump-er all round! For__ he is our glo-ry and pride; Our__ arms shall in bat-tle with

con-quest be crowned_ Whilst vir-tue and he's_ on our side.

'Tis Washington's health, loud can-
    nons should roar!
And trumpets the truth should
    proclaim;
There cannot be found, search all the
    world o'er,
His equal in virtue and fame.

'Tis Washington's health, our hero to
    bless,
May heaven look graciously down;
O long may he live, our hearts to
    possess,
And freedom still call him her own.

GOD SAVE THE THIRTEEN STATES

The victories of the new republic were inspiring to many Europeans. This is "a song made by a Dutch lady at The Hague, for the sailors of the five American vessels at Amsterdam." It was published in Philadelphia's Pennsylvania Packet in 1779. The melody is the familiar "God Save the King," a tune used for nearly a dozen English and American national anthems.

Majestically

God save the Thir - teen States! Long rule the U - nit - ed States!

God save our States! Make us vic - to - ri - ous, Hap - py and

glo - ri - ous; No ty - rants o - ver us; God save our States!

Oft did America
Foresee with sad dismay,
   Her slav'ry near.
Oft did her grievance state,
But Britain, falsely great,
Urging her desp'rate fate,
   Turned a deaf ear.

Now the proud British foe
We've made, by vict'ries, know
   Our sacred right.
Witness at Bunker's Hill,
Where godlike Warren fell,
Happy his blood to spill
   In gallant fight.

We'll fear no tyrant's nod
Nor stern oppression's rod,
   Till time's no more.
Thus Liberty, when driv'n
From Europe's states, is giv'n
A safe retreat and hav'n
   On our free shore.

O, Lord! Thy gifts in store,
We pray on Congress pour,
   To guide our States.
May union bless our land,
While we, with heart and hand,
Our mutual rights defend;
   God save our States!

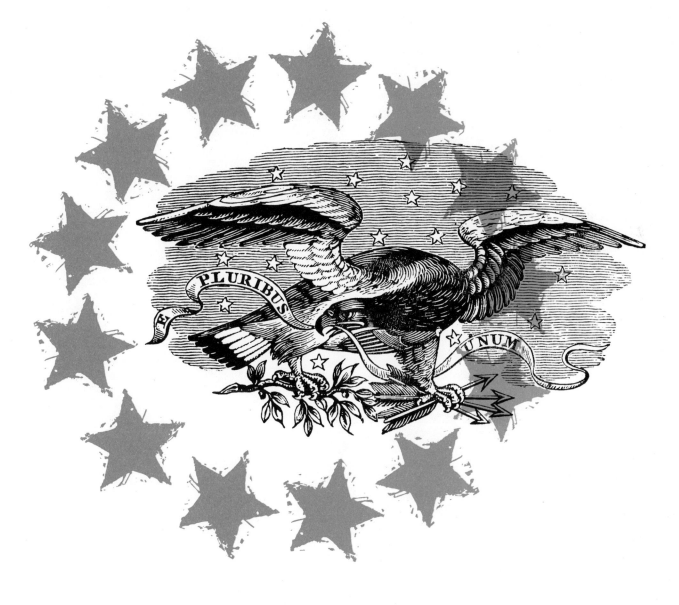

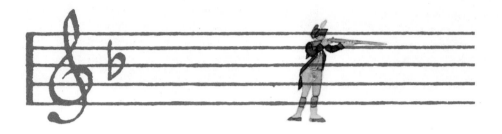

SERGEANT CHAMPE

In 1780, in order to award traitor Benedict Arnold his just desserts, General Washington enlisted the aid of Sergeant Champe of the dragoons. The sergeant was to pretend to desert the Americans and join up with the British in New York. Later, at a propitious moment, he was to assault Arnold and deliver him bound and gagged to Major Lee, who would be waiting across the Hudson on the Jersey shore. The plan was also devised as a method of clearing the English Major John André, who was implicated in Arnold's espionage and desertion.

Circumstances caused the scheme to be aborted in its final stages, and André's head was "gibbeted" as planned. Sergeant Champe later deserted the British and rejoined the American army, becoming a national hero when the details of the plot were made known.

In those days before the mass media, accounts of the news were often spread by broadside, and for those who could not read, by song. The following ballad, here abbreviated, recounted the story in complete and lengthy detail, for a people eager for news of the latest patriotic achievements. It is traditionally sung to the melody of "Barbara Allen," a seventeenth-century English song that has survived in over a hundred variations, in both England and America, down to the present day.

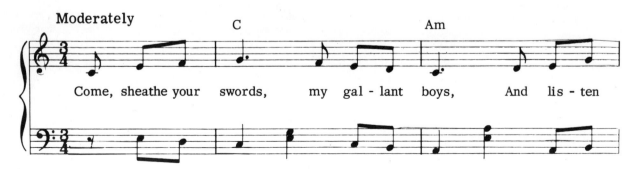

Come, sheathe your swords, my gal-lant boys, And lis-ten

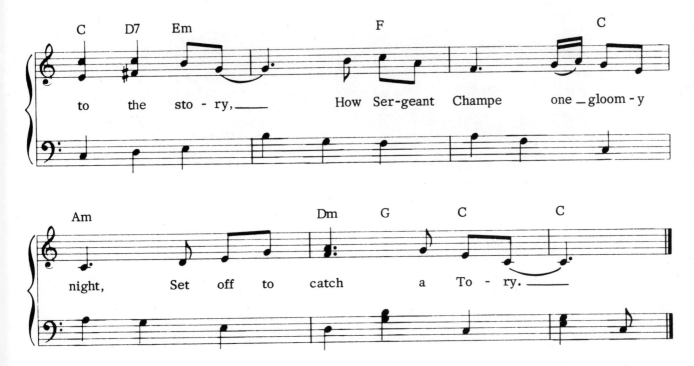

to the sto - ry, ___ How Ser-geant Champe one _ gloom - y night, Set off to catch a To - ry. ___

You see the gen'ral had got mad,
To think his plans were thwarted,
And swore by all, both good and bad,
That Arnold should be carted.

So unto Lee he sent a line,
And told him all his sorrow,
And said that he must start the hunt,
Before the coming morrow.

Lee found a sergeant in his camp,
Made up of bone and muscle,
Who ne'er knew fear, and many a
   year
With Tories had a tussle.

Bold Champe, when mounted on old
   Rip,
All buttoned up from weather,
Sang out, "Good-bye!" cracked off his
   whip,
And soon was in the heather.

At early morn, adown a hill
They saw the sergeant sliding;
So fast he went, it was not known,
Whether he's rode, or riding.

And so it happened that brave
   Champe
Unto Sir Hal deserted,
Deceiving him, and you, and me,
And into York was flirted.

He saw base Arnold in his camp,
Surrounded by the legion,
And told him of the recent prank
That threw him in that region.

Then Arnold grinned, and rubbed his
   hands,
And e'enmost choked with pleasure,
Not thinking Champe was all the
   while
A "taking of his measure."

Full soon the British fleet set sail!
Say! wasn't that a pity?
For thus it was brave Sergeant
   Champe
Was taken from the city.

To southern climes the shipping flew,
And anchored in Virginia,
When Champe escaped and joined
   his friends
Among the picininni.

Base Arnold's head, by luck, was
   saved,
Poor André's was gibbeted,
Arnold's to blame for André's fame,
And André's to be pitied.

CORNWALLIS
COUNTRY DANCE

This song, first published in 1781, describes the almost comic criss-crossing of South Carolina and North Carolina by Cornwallis in his attempts to find and destroy the Continentals under General Greene. Greene's smaller force utilized the guerrilla tactic of "hit and run" and so avoided a face-to-face confrontation. The campaign in the South became a chase, and the chase became a dance. When the dance was over in 1781, Cornwallis returned to Virginia.

The Washington referred to in verse 3 is William Washington, the general's cousin. The author of the text is unknown; the tune is the well-known "Yankee Doodle."

Corn-wal-lis led a coun-try dance, the like was nev-er seen, sir, Much ret-ro-grade and much ad-vance and all with Gen'-ral Greene, sir; They

ram - bled up and ram - bled down, joined hands and then they run, __ sir, Our

Gen' - ral Greene to Charles-town and the Earl to Wil - ming - ton, sir.

Greene, in the South, then danced a
    set,
      And got a mighty name, sir,
Cornwallis jigged with young Fayette,
      But suffered in his fame, sir;
Quoth he, "My guards are weary
    grown
      "With footing country dances,
"They never at St. James's shone
      "At capers, kicks, or prances."

And Washington, Columbia's son,
      Whom easy nature taught, sir,
That grace which can't by pains be
    won
      Nor Plutus' gold be bought, sir;

Now hand in hand they circle round,
      This ever-dancing peer, sir,
Their gentle movements soon
    confound
      The earl, as they draw near, sir.

His music soon forgets to play,
      His feet can no more move, sir,
And all his bands now curse the day
      They jiggéd to our shore, sir;
Now, Tories all, what can you say?
      Come, is not this a griper:
That while your hopes are danced
    away,
      'Tis you must pay the piper?

55

CORNWALLIS BURGOYNED

Of the many songs written to commemorate the defeat of the British army at Yorktown in 1781, "Cornwallis Burgoyned" was one of the more popular. The anonymous author used the melody of the Scottish song "Maggie Lauder," which was a great favorite among both the British and the American armies. Burgoyne, it will be recalled, was the British general who surrendered his entire command at Saratoga in 1777.

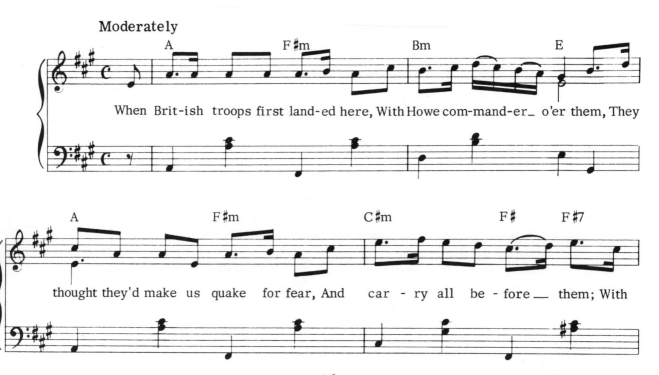

Moderately

When Brit-ish troops first land-ed here, With Howe com-mand-er_ o'er them, They thought they'd make us quake for fear, And car - ry all be - fore_ them; With

thir - ty thou-sand men or more And she with-out_ as - sist - ance, A-

mer - i - ca must needs give o'er, And make no more re-sist - ance.

But Washington, her glorious son,
    Of British hosts the terror,
Soon, by repeated overthrows,
    Convinced them of their error;
Let Princeton and let Trenton tell,
    What gallant deeds he's done,
        sir,
And Monmouth's plains where hun-
    dreds fell,
    And thousands more have run,
        sir.

When he sat down before the town,
    His Lordship soon surrendered,
His martial pride he laid aside,
    And cased the British standard;

Gods! How this stroke will North
    provoke,
    And all his thoughts confuse, sir!
And how the Peers will hang their
    ears,
    When first they hear the news,
        sir.

Be peace, the glorious end of war,
    By this event effected;
And be the name of Washington,
    To lastest times respected;
Then let us toast America,
    And France in union with her,
And may Great Britain rue the day
    Her hostile bands came hither.

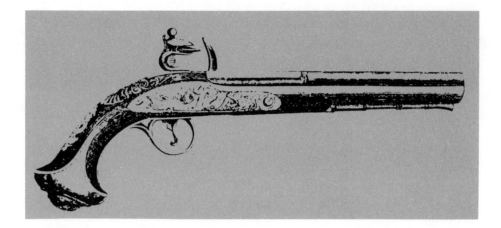

THE WORLD TURNED
UPSIDE DOWN

The decisive victory for the Americans was the surrender of Cornwallis at Yorktown on October 20, 1781, just four years after the defeat of Burgoyne at Saratoga. In the afternoon of that day, the sullen redcoats surrendered their weapons, while, so the story goes, the British bands struck up an appropriate tune, "The World Turned Upside Down."

The text of the song was originally published in the Gentleman's Magazine in London in 1767, with the subtitle "The Old Woman Taught Wisdom." It later appeared on a music sheet set to a popular English tune, "Down Derry Down" (see "What a Court Hath Old England" for another version of this tune). The anonymous author of the verses wrote that it was "an humble attempt to reconcile the parent and her children, made by a peace-maker to Great Britain and her Colonies." "Farmer Pitt," mentioned in verses 4 and 5, refers to William Pitt, the head of the British ministry at the time of publication and an avid pro-American.

Good-y Bull and her daugh-ter to - geth - er fell out. Both __

squab-bled and wran-gled and made a great rout! But the
cause of the quar-rel re-mains to be told, Then lend both your ears and a
tale I'll un-fold. Der-ry down, down, hey, der-ry down, Then
lend both your ears and a tale I'll un-fold.

The old lady, it seems, took a freak
   in her head,
That her daughter, grown woman,
   might earn her own bread;
Self-applauding her scheme, she was
   ready to dance,
But we're often too sanguine in what
   we advance.
     Derry down, down, hey, derry
     down,
But we're often too sanguine in what
   we advance.

For mark the event—thus for fortune
   we're crossed,
Nor should people reckon without
   their good host;
The daughter was sulky and wouldn't
   come to,
And pray what in this case could the
   old woman do?
     Derry down, down, hey, derry
     down,
And pray what in this case could the
   old woman do?

"Zounds! Neighbor," quoth Pitt, "what the devil's the matter?
"A man cannot rest in his home for your clatter."
"Alas!" cries the daughter. "Here's dainty fine work,
"The old woman grows harder than Jew or than Turk."
 Derry down, down, hey, derry down.
"The old woman grows harder than Jew or than Turk."

"She be damned!" says the farmer, and to her he goes,
First roars in her ears, then tweaks her old nose;
"Hello, Goody, what ails you? Wake, woman, I say,

"I am come to make peace in this desperate fray."
 Derry down, down, hey, derry down,
"I am come to make peace in this desperate fray."

"Alas!" cries the old woman. "And must I comply?
"But I'd rather submit than the hussy should die!"
"Pooh, prithee, be quiet, be friends and agree,
"You must surely be right if you're guided by me."
 Derry down, down, hey, derry down,
"You must surely be right if you're guided by me."

60

THE FEDERAL CONSTITUTION
AND LIBERTY FOREVER

The adoption of the Federal Constitution in 1788 provided an excellent subject for many of the country's songwriters. Even James Hewitt (1770–1827), who was born in England and did not arrive in America until 1792, utilized the event by composing the music for this song. The words were written by a Mr. Milns, a minor English playwright who came to New York in 1796. The song, first published around 1798, incorporates two famous melodies: in the first two bars, the theme of a popular military air, "Washington's March at the Battle of Trenton," and immediately following the change in meter, the melody of "Yankee Doodle."

Po - ets may sing of their Hel - i - con streams, Their

gods_ and their he - roes are fab - u - lous dreams, Their gods_ and their he - roes are

fab - u - lous dreams; They ne'er sang a line half so grand, so di-vine, As the

glo - ri - ous toast we Co - lum - bi-ans boast! The Fed-'ral Con-sti - tu-tion, boys, and

lib-er-ty for - ev - er, The Fed-'ral Con-sti - tu-tion, boys, and lib-er-ty for - ev - er.

A free navigation, commerce, and
    trade,
We'll seek for no foe, of no foe be
    afraid,
We'll seek for no foe, of no foe be
    afraid;
Our frigates shall ride, our defense
    and our pride,
Our tars guard our coast and huzza
    for our toast:
The Federal Constitution, trade, and
    commerce, boys, forever,
The Federal Constitution, trade, and
    commerce, boys, forever.

Fame's trumpet shall swell in Wash-
    ington's praise,
And time grant a furlough to lengthen
    his days,
And time grant a furlough to lengthen
    his days;
May health weave the thread of de-
    light round his head;
No nation can boast such a name—
    such a toast;
The Federal Constitution, boys, and
    Washington forever,
The Federal Constitution, boys, and
    Washington forever.

ODE FOR AMERICAN INDEPENDENCE

The Fourth of July in 1789 was an occasion for celebration in the United States. A nation had been born, and the Constitution was ratified. To mark the first observance of the signing of the Declaration of Independence, this song was written, with words by Daniel George and music by Horatio Garnet. It was also known as "Ode to the Fourth of July."

'Tis done, the e - dict passed, by Heav - en de - creed,__ And Han - cock's _____ name con - firms the

65

shore to shore let can - nons roar! And _

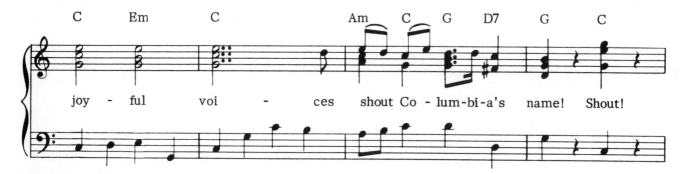

joy - ful voi - ces shout Co - lum-bi-a's name! Shout!

Shout Co-lum-bi-a's name, Co - lum - bi - a's name!

Now shall the useful arts of peace
    prevail,
And commerce flourish—favored by
    each gale;
        Discord forever cease,
        Let liberty and peace
        And justice reign;
For Washington protects the scientific
    train.
Chorus:

HAIL, COLUMBIA!

The words of "Hail, Columbia!" were written in 1798 by Joseph Hopkinson, son of the composer Francis Hopkinson, to the music of "The President's March," a popular instrumental piece composed by Philip Phile in 1793 or 1794. Hopkinson wrote the song to assist his friend Gilbert Fox, an actor, who wished to attract a large audience by the rendition of this popular piece. The author later explained that he hoped the lyrics would "get up an American spirit," which should be "above the interests" of both political parties of the day. "Hail, Columbia!" gained widespread popularity and became a national song in a surprisingly short time.

With dignity

Hail, Co-lum-bia, hap-py land! Hail! ye he-roes, heav'n born band, Who

fought and bled in free-dom's cause, Who fought and bled in free-dom's cause, And

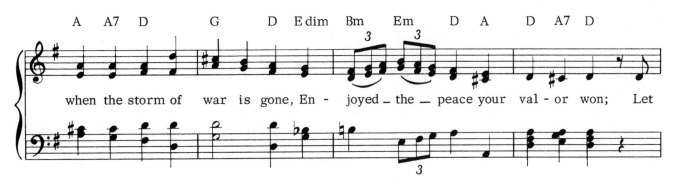

when the storm of war is gone, En - joyed _ the _ peace your val - or won; Let

in - de-pen-dence be _ your _ boast, Ev - er mind-ful what it costs;

Ev - er grate-ful for _ the _ prize, Let its al - tar reach the skies.

Chorus:

Firm, u - nit - ed, let _ us _ be, Ral - lying round our lib - er - ty,

As a band of _ broth-ers _ joined, Peace _ and _ safe - ty we shall find.

Immortal patriots! rise once more,
Defend your rights, defend your shore;
Let no rude foe with impious hand,
Let no rude foe with impious hand,
Invade the shrine where sacred lies
Of toil and blood the well-earned
    prize;

While off'ring peace, sincere and just,
In heav'n we place a manly trust:
That truth and justice will prevail,
And ev'ry scheme of bondage fail.
Chorus:

Sound, sound the trump of fame!
Let Washington's great name
Ring through the world with loud
    applause!
Ring through the world with loud
    applause!
Let ev'ry clime to freedom dear
Listen with a joyful ear;

With equal skill, with godlike pow'r,
He governs in the fearful hour
Of horrid war, or guides with ease
The happier times of honest peace.
Chorus:

WE THE PEOPLE C
IN ORDER TO FOR
ESTABLISH JUSTI
PROVIDE FOR THE
THE GENERAL WE
BLESSINGS OF LII

HUZZA FOR LIBERTY

This rousing Yankee drinking song was published in 1798, two years after its author, George K. Jackson (1745–1823), arrived in Norfolk, Virginia, from England. Jackson's First Principles, or A Treatise on Practical Thorough Bass *had established him in England as a competent and knowledgeable musician. He eventually secured the position of organist at the Haydn and Handel Society in Boston, where for a time he exerted considerable musical influence.*

Come, lads, your glass-es fill with glee, And drink a health to

lib - er - ty; Huz- za, Huz-za, Huz- za! Huz- za, Huz-za, Huz-

za! Huz- za, Huz-za, Huz- za! za!

Hail, ye heroes, wise and bold,
To future times your names be told;
Huzza, Huzza, Huzza!
Huzza, Huzza, Huzza!

Youth descended from such sires,
Feed, feed, feed, feed the sacred fires;
Huzza, Huzza, Huzza!
Huzza, Huzza, Huzza!

The fires which warm Columbia's
    race,
And shine with luster in each face;
Huzza, Huzza, Huzza!
Huzza, Huzza, Huzza!

Free-born sons no chains will bear,
But those of love we'll gladly wear;
Huzza, Huzza, Huzza!
Huzza, Huzza, Huzza!

A FUNERAL DIRGE ON THE DEATH OF GENERAL GEORGE WASHINGTON

The eighteenth century came to an end, marked by the death of George Washington on December 14, 1799. A period of mourning followed, and finally his burial on February 22, 1800. General Washington had been a great force in establishing the United States, and the people were grateful to him for it.

To many he was a giant among men, as is testified by such songs as this. Written by Peter Albrecht von Hagen (1750–1803), organist of the Stone Chapel in Boston, it was published in January of 1800.

The title page of one edition depicts an urn, with the inscription:

> *G. W. Born Feb. 22, 1732.*
> *Died at Mount Vernon, Dec. 14, 1799.*
> *Aged 68.*

At the urn's base is written: "The just shall be had in everlasting remembrance."

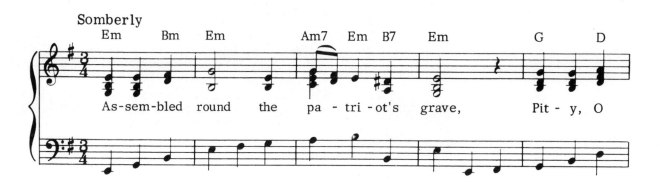

Somberly

As-sem-bled round the pa - tri - ot's grave, Pit - y, O

Lord, a na - tion's sighs, We mourn our chief, the war - ri - or brave; Low in the dust the he - ro lies.

His country happy, great, and free,
Hailed him her father, hope, and
    pride;
But fixed, O God, his hope on thee,
He lived thy friend, thy servant died.

MOUNT-VERNON

Written by the Connecticut composer Stephen Jenks (1772–1856), this song was "Composed on the death of Gen'l Washington" and was published in Jenks's The New England Harmony *in 1800. The book contained "concise and easy rules of music together with a number of tunes adapted to public worship, most of which were never before published." Jenks, who compiled a number of similar songbooks, spent the last twenty-five years of his life as a drum and tambourine maker in Thompson, Ohio.*

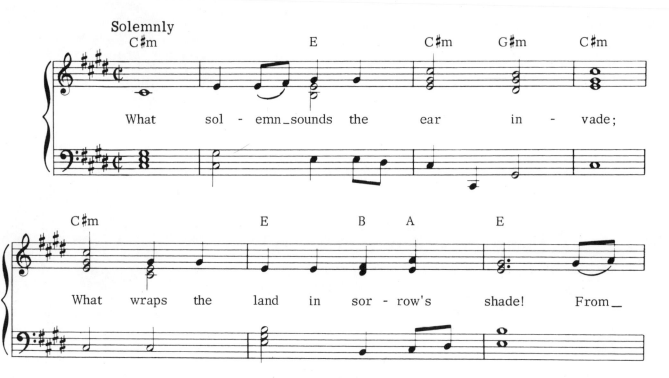

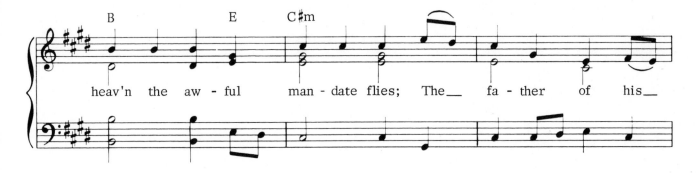

heav'n the aw - ful man - date flies; The__ fa - ther of his__

coun - try__ dies. Where shall our coun - try

turn its eye? What help re - mains be - neath the sky!

Our friend, pro - tec - tor, strength, and trust Lies

low and mold - er - ing in the dust. dust.

II
Ballads and Other Popular Songs

MY DAYS HAVE BEEN
SO WONDROUS FREE

This song until recently has been considered the first composition by a native American. Current musical scholarship now tends to give the honor to John Tufts for his "100 Psalm Tune New"; but the following song remains, in all probability, the first secular American composition. It is the work of Francis Hopkinson (1737–1791), writer, musician, poet, painter, man of society, signer of the Declaration of Independence, and practicing lawyer. Hopkinson's suave and urbane life-style is particularly reflected in this song, composed in 1759. The words are by the English poet Thomas Parnell (1679–1718), from his "Love and Innocence."

My days have been so wondrous free, The little birds that fly with careless ease from tree to tree were

but as blest as I, were but as blest as I;

Ask glid - ing wa - ters if a

tear of mine in - creased their stream, And ask the breath-ing

gales if e'er I lent a sigh to them, I

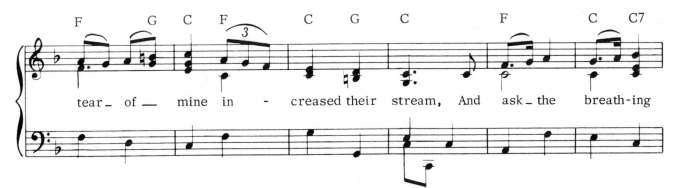

lent a sigh to them.

COLLINET AND PHEBE

The lyrics to this anonymous ballad, quite popular among the colonists, were first printed in the Pennsylvania Magazine in 1776, and were reprinted occasionally in the newspapers as the war progressed. Here patriotic fervor infuses the text of a sentimental ballad, and a young woman's devotion to her country takes precedence over love. The tune for which the text was written, "As Jamie Gay Blithe Gang'd his Way," was first printed in London in 1760, and reappeared frequently in sheet music on this side of the Atlantic.

love. "Dear bloom - ing maid," the shep - herd_ said, "My

ten - der_ vow_____ be - lieve; These_ down - cast_ eyes and

art - less_____ sighs, Can_ ne'er thy faith_____ de - ceive."

"Though some there are, from fair to fair,
　　"Delighting wild to rove,
"Such change thou ne'er from me canst fear,
　　"Thy charms secure my love.
"Then Phebe, now, approve my vow,
　　"By truth, by fondness pressed;
"Smile, assume to grace thy bloom,
　　"And make thy shepherd blessed."

A blush o'erspread her cheek with red,
　　Which half she turned aside;
With pleasing woes, her bosom rose,
　　And thus the maid replied:
"Dear gentle youth, I know thy truth,
　　"And all thy arts to please;
"But, ah, is this a time for bliss,
　　"Or themes as soft as these?"

"While all around we hear no sound,
　　"But war's terrible strains!
"The drum commands our arming bands,
　　"And chides each tardy swain.
"Our country's call arouses all
　　"Who dare be brave and free!
"My love shall crown the youth alone
　　"Who saves himself and me."

" 'Tis done!" he cried, "From thy dear side,
　　"Now quickly I'll be gone;
"From love will I, to freedom fly,
　　"A slave to thee alone.
"And when I come with laurels home,
　　"And all that freemen crave,
"To crown my love, your smiles shall prove,
　　"The fair reward the brave."

JOHNNY HAS GONE
FOR A SOLDIER

The struggle and sorrow occasioned by the Revolutionary War were rarely acknowledged in song—perhaps because patriotic devotion and military zeal were felt to be more virtuous sentiments. "The American Hero" (earlier in this book) is one exception, and the beautiful "Johnny Has Gone for a Soldier" is another. This anonymous ballad, based on the eighteenth-century Irish folk tune "Shule Aroon," has remained in currency since it was first written. It has periodically returned to popularity during later times of struggle, particularly during the Civil War.

Slowly

Here I sit on But-ter-milk Hill, Who could blame me,

cry my fill? And ev - 'ry tear would —

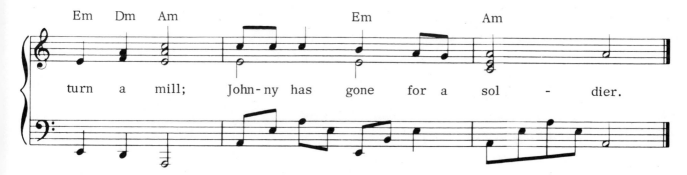

turn a mill; John-ny has gone for a sol - dier.

Me, oh, my, I loved him so,
Broke my heart to see him go,
And only time will heal my woe;
Johnny has gone for a soldier.

I'll sell my clock, I'll sell my reel,
Likewise I'll sell my spinning wheel
To buy my love a sword of steel;
Johnny has gone for a soldier.

HOW HAPPY THE SOLDIER

Here's a light-hearted, easy-going tune that plays up the carefree aspect of military life. Its tone is in remarkable contrast to the preceding song—perhaps because it was written after the war had ended. The song is from The Poor Soldier, *a comic opera by William Shield and John O'Keefe first performed in Dublin in 1783 and later in the United States—and one of George Washington's favorites. This particular song seems to have been more popular on this side of the Atlantic than in England.*

How hap - py the sol - dier who lives on his pay, And spends half a crown out of six-pence a day; Yet fears nei - ther jus - tic - es,

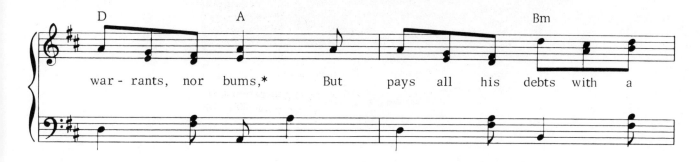

war - rants, nor bums,* But pays all his debts with a

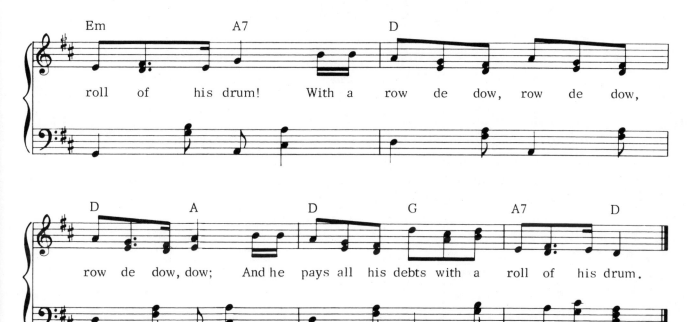

roll of his drum! With a row de dow, row de dow,

row de dow, dow; And he pays all his debts with a roll of his drum.

*Short for "bumbailiffs," bailiffs used in arrests and consequently the meanest and most feared.

He cares not a marnedy how the world goes,
His King finds his quarters and money and clothes;
He laughs at all sorrow whenever it comes,
And rattles away with a roll of his drum!
With a row de dow, row de dow, row de dow, dow!
And rattles away with a roll of his drum.

The drum is his glory, his joy, his delight,
It leads him to pleasure as well as to fight;
No girl, when she hears it, though ever so glum,
But packs up her tatters and follows the drum.
With a row de dow, row de dow, row de dow, dow;
But packs up her tatters and follows the drum.

ANACREONTIC SONG

The official song of the Anacreontic Society of London, celebrating the delights of wine and women, has words by Ralph Tomlinson and music by an unknown composer. The song was first published in London around 1779 or 1780 and was an instant success. The inspiring melody provided the basis for a large number of American parodies, among them lyrics by such notables as Francis Hopkinson, Thomas Paine, and Francis Scott Key. At least eighty-five versions of the song were located at the last counting.

To A - na - cre - on in heav'n, where he sat in full glee, A few sons of har - mo - ny sent a pe - ti - tion,__ That he their in - spir - er and pa - tron would

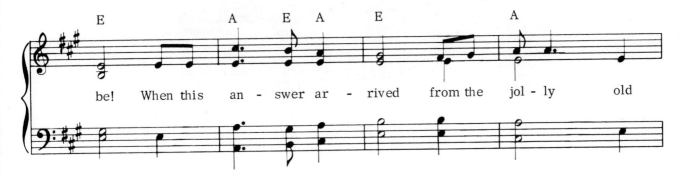

be! When this an - swer ar - rived from the jol - ly old

Gre-cian:"Voice, fid-dle, and flute, No _ long-er be mute! I'll _

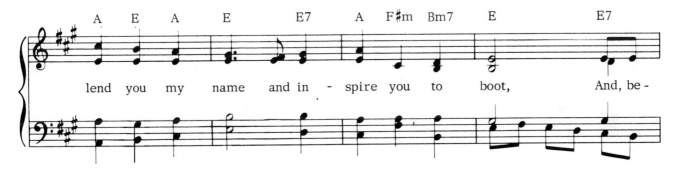

lend you my name and in - spire you to boot, And, be -

sides, I'll in - struct you like me to _ en - twine _ The

Myr - tle of _ Ve - nus with Bac - chus - 's _ vine!"

COME, FAIR ROSINA

In 1788 Francis Hopkinson published a collection entitled Seven Songs for the Harpsichord or Forte piano. *It was dedicated "to his excellency George Washington, Esquire" and was accompanied by the following inscription:*

> *I embrace, with heart-felt satisfaction, every opportunity that offers of recognizing the personal Friendship that hath so long subsisted between us. The present Occasion allows me to do this in a manner most flattering to my Vanity; and I have accordingly taken advantage of it, by presenting this Work to your Patronage, and honouring it with your name. . . .*
>
> *However small the Reputation may be that I shall derive from this Work, I cannot, I believe, be refused the Credit of being the first Native of the United States who has produced a Musical Composition. If this attempt should not be too severely treated, others may be encouraged to venture on a path, yet untrodden in America, and the Arts in succession will take root and flourish amongst us.*

"Come, Fair Rosina" is the first song in the collection.

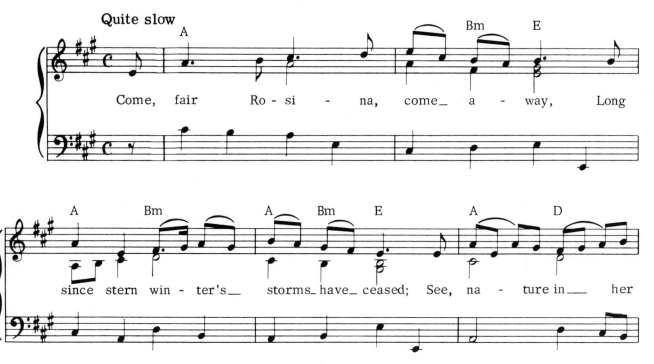

91

o - dors shed and__ ev - 'ry breeze_____ pours_

fra - grance_ down.

At noon we'll seek the wild wood's
  shade,
And o'er the pathless verdure rove;
Or, near a mossy fountain laid,
Attend the music of the grove;
At eve, the sloping mead invites

With lowing herds, with lowing
  herds and flocks to stray,
Each hour shall furnish new delights,
And love and joy shall crown the day;
Each hour shall furnish new delights,
And love and joy shall crown the day.

MY LOVE IS GONE TO SEA

After receiving the collection, George Washington sent Hopkinson a gracious letter accepting the dedication:

My dear Sir, if you had any doubts about the reception which your work would meet with—or had the smallest reason to think that you should meet with any assistance to defend it—you have not acted with your usual good judgment in the choice of a coadjutator, for . . . what alas! can I do to support it? I can neither sing one of the songs, nor raise a note on any instrument to convince the unbelieving. But I have, however, one argument which will prevail with persons of true estate (at least in America)—I can tell them that it is the production of Mr. Hopkinson.

My_ love is gone to sea, While I his ab-sence mourn, No_ joy shall smile on me____ un-til my love_ re - turn;__ He_ asked me for his

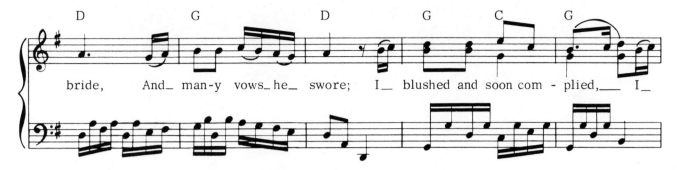

bride, And_ man-y vows_he_ swore; I_ blushed and soon com - plied,___ I_

blushed and soon com - plied,___ My heart was his_ be - fore,____ My

heart was his, my heart was his_ be - fore.____

One little month was past
And who so blest as we?
The summons came at last,
And Jemmy must to sea;
I saw his ship so gay
Swift fly the wave-worn shore;
I wiped my tears away,
And saw his ship no more,
No more, no more,
And saw his ship no more.

When clowds shut in the sky
And storms around me howl,
When livid lightnings fly
And threat'ning thunders roll,
All hopes of rest are lost,
No slumbers visit me;
My anxious thoughts are tossed
With Jemmy on the sea;
My thoughts are tossed
With Jemmy on the sea.

BENEATH A WEEPING
WILLOW'S SHADE

Hopkinson's choice of subject matter throughout the collection reflects a strong English influence. This song is one of the more popular ones from his collection.

Be - neath a weep - ing wil - low's shade she sat and sang a -

lone; Be - neath a weep - ing wil - low's shade she sat and sang a -

lone; Her hand up-on — her heart — she laid, and plain-tive was — her

moan, and plain-tive was — her moan. — The — mock-ing bird sat up-

on — a bough, The — mock-ing bird sat up-

on — a bough, And lis-tened to — her lay; — then to the dis-tant

hills — he bore — the dul-cet notes — a-way; Then to the dis-tant

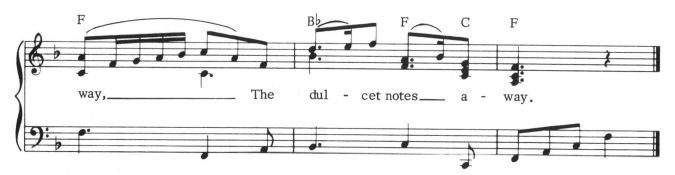

hills_ he bore the dul - cet notes a - way,_____ The dul - cet notes a - way,_____ The dul - cet notes___ a - way.

Fond echo to her strains replied,
The winds her sorrows bore;
"Adieu, dear youth, adieu," she cried,
"I ne'er shall see thee more."
Chorus:

RONDO

The seventh song in the dedication collection, "Rondo," illustrates Hopkinson's musical sophistication. The accompaniment patterns show his familiarity with popular European composers.

My__ gen'-rous heart dis - dains the__ slave of love to

be; I__ scorn his ser-vile chains and__ boast my lib-er-

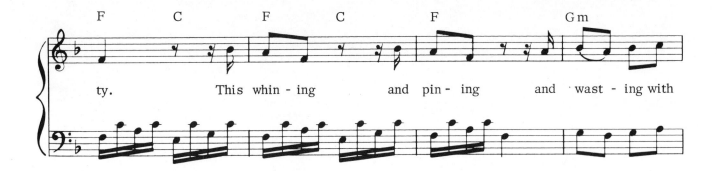

ty. This whin - ing and pin - ing and wast - ing with

care are__ not to my__ taste,__ be she ev - er so fair.

Fine

Shall a girl's ca - pri - cious_frown sink my no - ble___

spir - its___ down? Shall a face _ of ___

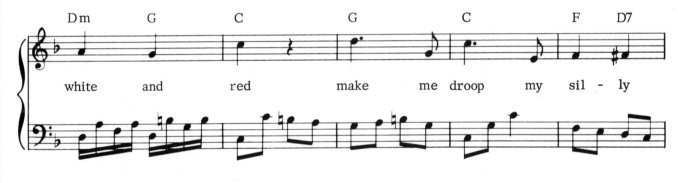

white and red make me droop my sil - ly

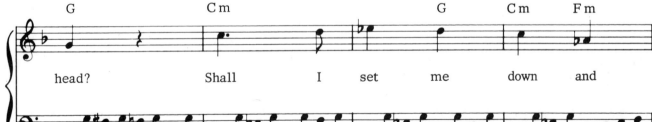

head? Shall I set me down and

sigh for an eye - brow___ or ___ an___

eye?   For   a   braid - ed   lock   of

hair?   Curse_ my_   for - tune,   curse_ my_   for - tune

and des - pair;   Curse my_   for - tune_ and_ des - pair.

*D. C. al 𝄋 **

Still   un - cer - tain   is   to -

mor - row,   Not   quite   cer - tain_ is_   to - day,

*Play first 15 bars again and then continue from this point.

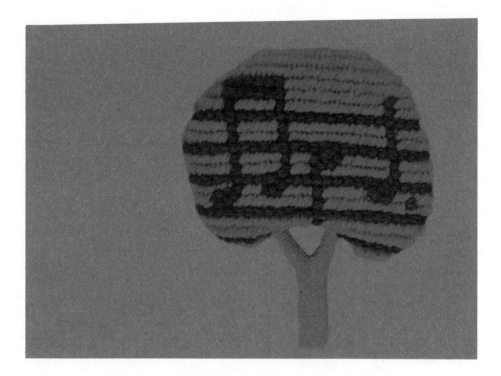

WHILST THROUGH
THE SHARP HAWTHORN

In the collection Seven Songs *dedicated to George Washington by Francis Hopkinson, this is the eighth song. A footnote explains: "N.B. This Eighth Song was added after the Title Page was engraved."*

Hopkinson sent a copy of the collection to Thomas Jefferson, noting that the last song, "if played very slow, and sung with Expression, is forcibly pathetic—at least in my fancy." Jefferson replied: "While my elder daughter was playing it on a harpsichord, I happened to look toward the fire and saw the younger one all in tears. I asked if she was sick? She said 'No; but the tune was so mournful.'"

Slowly, with expression

The trav'-ler be-night-ed and lost,___ O'er the moun-tain pur-sues his lone

way,   The stream is all can-died with frost,   And the i-ci-cle hangs on the

spray;   He wan-ders in hope some kind   shel-ter to find, Whilst_

through the sharp haw-thorn still blows the cold wind;   He wan-ders in hope some kind

shel-ter to find, Whilst_ through the sharp haw-thorn still blows the cold wind.

The tempest howls dreary around
And rends the tall oak in its flight;
Fast falls the cold snow on the ground,
And dark is the gloom of the night.
Lone wanders the trav'ler a shelter to find
Whilst through the sharp hawthorn still blows the cold wind;
Lone wanders the trav'ler a shelter to find
Whilst through the sharp hawthorn still blows the cold wind.

No comfort the wild woods afford,
No shelter the trav'ler can see—
Far off are his bed and his board
And his home, where he wishes to be.
His hearth's cheerful blaze still engages his mind
Whilst through the sharp hawthorn still blows the cold wind;
His hearth's cheerful blaze still engages his mind
Whilst through the sharp hawthorn still blows the cold wind.

DRINK TO ME ONLY

This familiar English drinking song, still a favorite today, was heard often in the colonies. It was arranged for piano by Alexander Reinagle (1756–1809) and included in his book A Collection of Favorite Songs (Philadelphia, 1789). Although Reinagle did not arrive in America until after his thirtieth birthday, his composing and conducting activities soon gained him musical prominence. This setting of Ben Jonson's poem demonstrates his grasp of traditional compositional techniques.

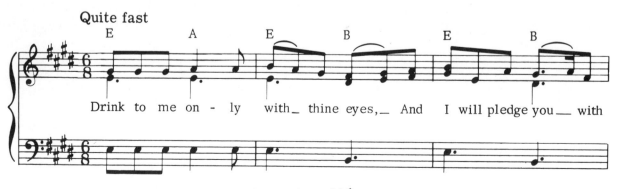

Drink to me on - ly with_ thine eyes,_ And I will pledge you _ with

mine; Or leave a kiss with - in___ the cup,___ And I'll___ not ask___ for wine. The thirst___ that from the soul___ doth rise Doth ask a drink___ di - vine,_____ But might I of Love's nec - tar sip,___ I would___ not change___ for thine.

DEATH SONG OF AN INDIAN CHIEF

This song, "taken from Ouábi, an Indian tale, in four cantos, by Philenia, a lady of Boston," is distinguished as being the first orchestral score printed in the United States. It was distributed as an insert in The Massachusetts Magazine *for March, 1791. The composer was Hans Gram, organist of the Brattle Square Church in Boston. The piece was scored by Gram for strings, two clarinets, and two E-flat horns; it is here arranged for piano. The "lady of Boston" who wrote the text was Sarah Wentworth Morton.*

Reared midst the war em-pur-pled plain, What Il-li-nois sub-mits____ to pain; Reared_ midst the war em-pur-pled plain, What

Il-li-nois sub-mits to pain! How can the glo-ry dart - ing

fire the cow-ard chill of death in - spire? The cow-ard chill of

death in - spire? The cow-ard chill of death in - spire?

The sun a blazing heat bestows,
The moon midst pensive evening
   glows;
The stars in sparkling beauty shine,
And own their flaming source divine.

Then let me hail the immortal fire,
And in the sacred flames expire!
Nor yet those Huron hands restrain,
This bosom scorns the throbs of pain.

No griefs this warrior-foul can bow,
No pangs contract this even brow;
Not all your threats excite a fear,
Not all your force can start a tear.

Think not with me my tribe decays,
More glorious chiefs the hachet raise;
Not unrevenged their sachem dies,
Not unattended greets the skies.

OH, DEAR, WHAT CAN THE MATTER BE?

This English children's tune, by an unknown composer, was popular in the United States during the 1790s, and was even performed in theaters in New York and Philadelphia. The exact date of first publication is unknown; it is first found in print in Elegant Extracts for the Guitar, *Vol. 2, which appeared in London sometime between 1778 and 1787.*

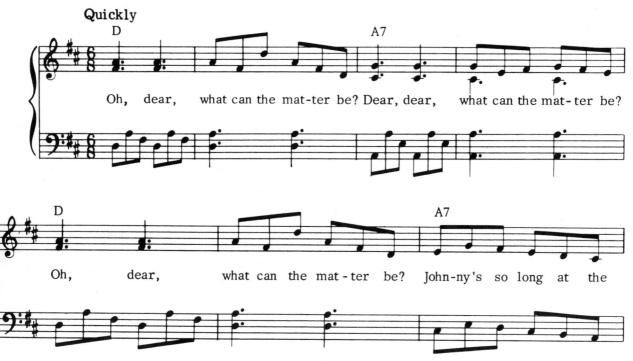

Oh, dear, what can the mat-ter be? Dear, dear, what can the mat-ter be?

Oh, dear, what can the mat - ter be? John-ny's so long at the

And now, oh, dear, what can the
    matter be?
Dear, dear, what can the matter be?
Oh, dear, what can the matter be?
Johnny's so long at the fair.

He promised he'd buy me a basket of
    posies,
A garland of lilies, a garland of roses,

A little straw hat to set off the blue
    ribbons
That tie up my bonny brown hair.

And now, oh, dear, what can the
    matter be?
Dear, dear, what can the matter be?
Oh, dear, what can the matter be?
Johnny's so long at the fair.

PRIMROSES

In the 1790s, large numbers of European musicians began arriving in America. Among them was James Hewitt, violinist, composer, conductor, and publisher, and already a seasoned professional when he arrived from England in 1792 at the age of 22.

Hewitt quickly established himself in New York by organizing concerts and conducting. This included directing outdoor summer concerts where, for the price of admission, the listener was entitled to free ice cream and an exhibition of fireworks.

"Primroses" (also known as "The Primrose Girl") was published one year after its composer had arrived in this country. It was so popular that within two years it was issued by seven different firms. This version was described as "a favorite song sung by Mrs. Pownall, with additions and alterations by a Lady."

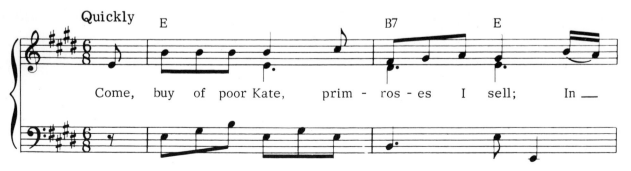

Come, buy of poor Kate, prim - ros - es I sell; In —

Lon-don's famed cit-y I'm known ver-y well; _ Tho' my heart is quite sunk yet I con-stant-ly cry: Come, who'll buy _ prim - ros - es? _ Come, _ who'll buy _ prim -ros - es? _ Come, _ who'll buy prim-ros-es? Who'll _ buy? Who'll buy?

Friends and parents I've none, I am
    looked on with scorn,
Ah, better for me that I ne'er had
    been born;
Here I sue for protection while plain-
    tive I cry:
Come, who'll buy primroses? Come,
    who'll buy primroses?
        Who'll buy? Who'll buy?

My companions despise me and say
    I am proud,
Because I avoid them and keep from
    their crowd;

For wicked temptations I ever will fly,
I live by primroses: Come, who'll buy
    primroses?
        Who'll buy? Who'll buy?

If pity to virtue were ever allied,
The tear of compassion ne'er yet was
    denied;
Then pity poor Kate who plaintive
    doth cry:
Come, who'll buy primroses? Come,
    who'll buy primroses?
        Who'll buy? Who'll buy?

113

ALKNOMOOK

Subtitled "The Death Song of the Cherokee Indians" and originally published in England in 1784, this song was known on both sides of the Atlantic. The words were written by Anne Home Hunter, the wife of an English physician who had spent time in America as an army surgeon under Burgoyne. In 1794, Mrs. Hunter revealed the source of the music: "The simple melody for this song was brought to England ten years ago by a gentleman named Turner, who had spent nine years amongst the natives of America. He assured the author that it was peculiar to that tribe or nation called the Cherokees, and that they chanted it to a barbarous jargon, implying contempt for their enemies in the moments of torture and death."

The sun sets at night, and the stars shun the day; But their

glo - ry re - mains when their light fades a-way. Be - gin, ye tor-men-tors,your

threats are in vain, For the son of Alk-no-mook will nev - er com-plain.

Remember the arrows he shot from
his bow?
Remember the chiefs by his hatchet
laid low?
Why so slow—do you think I shall
shrink from the pain?
No, the son of Alknomook will never
complain.

Remember the woods where in am-
bush we lay?
And the scalps which we bore from
your nations away?
Now the flame rises high, you exult
in my pain,
But the son of Alknomook will scorn
to complain.

I go to the land where my father is
gone,
His ghost will rejoice at the fame of
his son;
Death comes like a saint to relieve me
from pain,
For the son of Alknomook would
never complain.

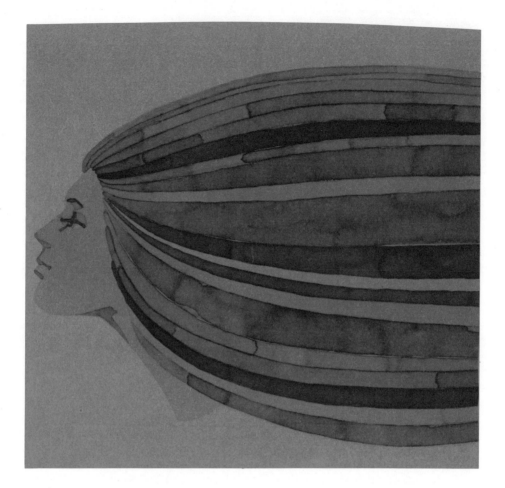

THE DREAM

"The Dream" was first published in 1794 by Carr and Company's Musical Repository in Philadelphia. The composer of the music is unknown. The text is by Ann Julia Hatton, who also wrote the libretto for James Hewitt's Tammany, *a controversial anti-Federalist opera commissioned by the political Tammany Society that included the preceding song in this anthology, "Alknomook."*

The oth - er day by sleep op - pressed as I a

The nymphs adorned the nuptial bow'r,
With ev'ry fragrant blooming flow'r;
And graceful smiling at my side
Young Edward stood, the village pride.

Pleased, I awoke, found Edward near,
Who quickly banished ev'ry fear;
O, love, thy blessings o'er me shed,
For I this night intend to wed.

AMERICA, COMMERCE, AND FREEDOM

Alexander Reinagle was one of a number of foreign-born musicians who came to dominate the American musical scene toward the end of the century. Born in Portsmouth, England, he began his musical career in Scotland and moved to New York in 1786, calling himself a "member of the Society of Musicians in London."

Reinagle eventually settled in Philadelphia, where his talents were soon appreciated. He became a music teacher to the best families; he conducted and performed in numerous concerts; and in addition he presided at the harpsichord at opera performances in several cities.

"America, Commerce, and Freedom," one of Reinagle's finer songs, was published in 1794, and was "sung by Mr. Darley Junr. in the Ballet Pantomine of the Sailor's Landlady."

scene — de-lights by chang - ing. Tho' tem - pests howl a -

long the main, Some ob - ject will __ re - mind us, And

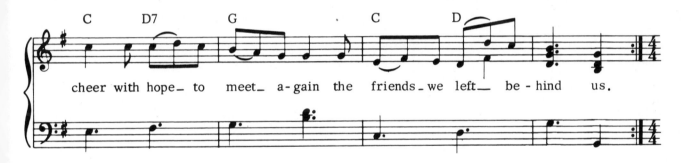

cheer with hope __ to meet __ a-gain the friends __ we left __ be - hind us.

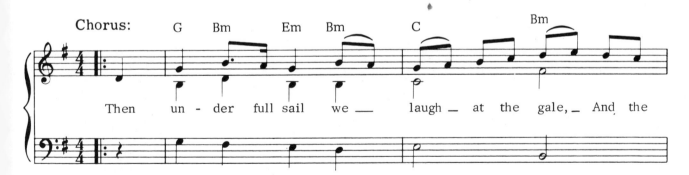

Chorus:

Then un - der full sail we __ laugh __ at the gale, __ And the

lands - men look pale — nev-er heed 'em; But toss off the glass to a

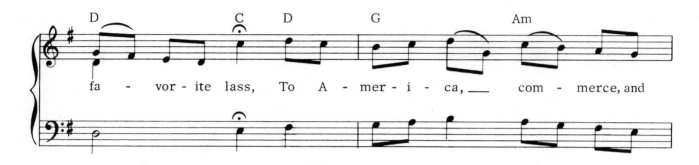

fa - vor - ite lass, To A - mer - i - ca, ___ com - merce, and

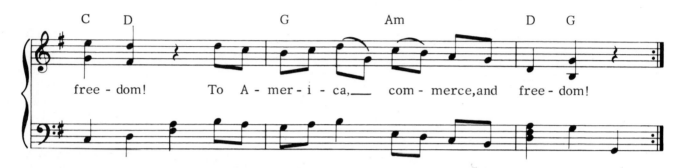

free - dom! To A - mer - i - ca, ___ com - merce, and free - dom!

But when arrived in sight of land
Or safe in port rejoicing,
Our ship we moor, our sails we hand,
Whilst out the boat is hoisting;
With cheerful hearts the shore we
    reach
Our friends delighted greet us,
And tripping lightly o'er the beach
The pretty lasses meet us.
Chorus:

A NEGRO SONG

"A Negro Song" was composed by Benjamin Carr (1768–1831), English-born composer, organist, pianist, concert manager, singer, and publisher. Carr came to the United States in 1793, at the age of 25, and soon established himself as the dominant musician in Philadelphia, capital of the new republic from 1790 to 1800 and the nucleus of American culture.

Published around 1800, the song was written after the following event, "verified by the Dutchess of Devonshire": "They lightened their labour by songs, one of which was composed extempore, for I was myself the subject of it. It was sung by one of the young women, the rest joining in a sort of chorus. The air was sweet and plaintive, and the words, literally translated, were these:

The winds roared, and the rains fell
The poor white man, faint and weary
Came and sat under our tree
He has no mother to bring him milk;
No wife to grind his corn.
(Chorus) Let us pity the white man;
No mother has he, &c,&c."

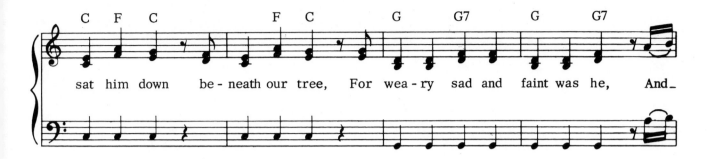

sat him down be-neath our tree, For wea-ry sad and faint was he, And_

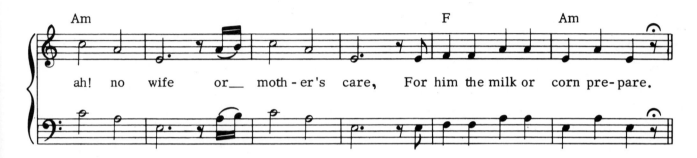

ah! no wife or_ moth-er's care, For him the milk or corn pre-pare.

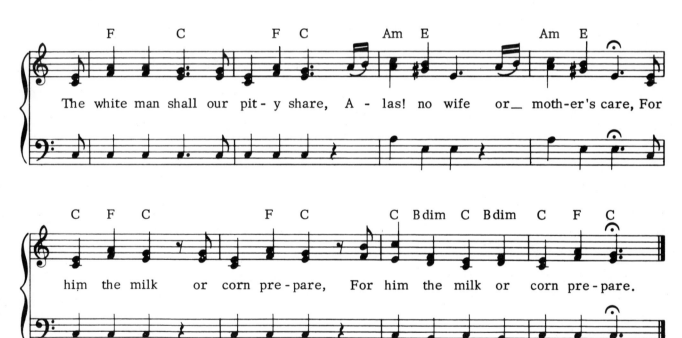

The white man shall our pit-y share, A - las! no wife or_ moth-er's care, For

him the milk or corn pre-pare, For him the milk or corn pre-pare.

The storm is o'er, the tempest past,
And mercy's voice has hushed the
    blast;
The wind is heard in whispers low,
The white man far away must go;
But ever in his heart will bear
Remembrance of the Negroes' care.

Go, white man, go, and with thee
    bear
The Negroes' wish, the Negroes'
    prayer,
Remembrance of the Negroes' care,
Remembrance of the Negroes' care.

III

Psalm-Tunes, Hymns, and Singing-School Songs

148th PSALM

The first book containing music notation to be printed in the English colonies was the ninth edition of the Bay Psalm Book, *printed in Boston in 1698. The title page reads in part:*

The Psalms, Hymns, and Spiritual Songs, of Old & New-Testament: Faithfully Translated into English Meetre.
For the use, Edification and Comfort of the Saints in publick and private, especially in New-England.

The book consists of thirteen psalm-tunes in two parts, printed with diamond-shaped notes (but no text) from crude woodcuts. The tunes were apparently those most popular in the colonies at the end of the seventeenth century. The one used here dates back to 1558; the text is from the first edition of the Bay Psalm Book, *which was printed in 1640—probably the first English-language book printed in America.*

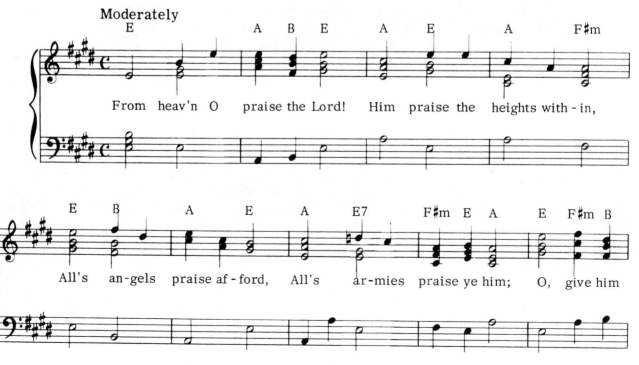

Moderately

From heav'n O praise the Lord! Him praise the heights with-in,

All's an-gels praise af-ford, All's ar-mies praise ye him; O, give him

praise! Sun and moon bright, All stars of light, O give him praise.

Ye heav'ns of heav'ns him praise,
O'er 'e heav'ns ye waters clear,
The Lord's name let them praise;
For he spake made they were:
Then stablisht he
For ever and aye
Nor shall away
His made decree.

Praise God from the earth below:
Ye dragons and each deep.
Fire and hail, mist and snow:
Whirlwinds his word which keep.
Mountains, also
You hills all ye:
Each fruitful tree,
All cedars, too.

MARTYRS TUNE

"Martyrs Tune" is one of thirteen tunes published in the 1698 edition of the Bay Psalm Book. The editors of that edition suggested that the tune be used for singing the Thirty-ninth Psalm, and they advised the singers to "begin your first note low." "Martyrs Tune" first appeared in print in Edinburgh in 1615. It is set here with three of the eleven verses of Psalm 39 from the Bay Psalm Book of 1640.

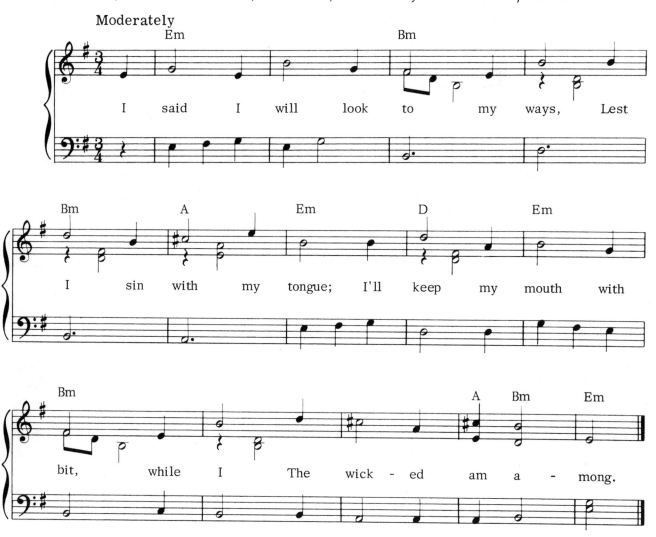

With silence tied was my tongue,
My mouth I did refrain
From speaking of that thing which is
    good,
And stirred was my pain.

Mine heart within me waxed hot,
While I was musing long;
Inkindled in me was the fire,
Then spake I with my tongue.

Mine end, O Lord, and of my days
Let me the measure learn;
That what a momentary thing
I am I may discern.

SOUTHWEL NEW

"*Southwel New,*" *possibly the first composition written by a native American, was published in 1721 in* Grounds and Rules of Musick Explained, *by the Reverend Thomas Walter (1696–1725) of Roxbury, Massachusetts. Walter's little book exerted considerable musical influence for many years. In it he advanced the controversial idea of teaching singers of church music "the just and equal Timing of the Notes." "The whole Assembly shall begin and end every single Note and every Line exactly together," he recommended, "which is a wonderful Beauty in singing. . . . But for want of this, I have observed in many Places one Man is upon this Note, while another is a Note before him, which produces something so hideous and disorderly, as is beyond Expression bad."*

Following a lengthy set of instructions to singers is a collection of tunes, all but one of which were taken from several earlier books. That exception, "Southwel New," is not known to have appeared in print previously, and so may have been written by Walter himself. The words to the song are from the Bay Psalm Book of 1640.

Moderately

Bow down, O Lord, thine ear, And hark - en un - to me;

Be - cause that I af - flict - ed am, al - so I am need - y.

Do thou preserve my soul,
　For gracious am I;
O thou, my God, thy servant save
　That doth on thee rely.

Lord, pity me for I
　Cry daily thee unto;
Rejoice thy servant's soul, for Lord
　To thee mine lift I do.

For thou, O Lord, art good,
　To pardon prone withal;
And to them all in mercy rich
　That do upon thee call.

131

100 PSALM TUNE NEW

This setting of Psalm 100 is one of the earliest known musical compositions by a native American. Probably written by the Reverend John Tufts (1689–1752), it was included in the fifth edition of his book An Introduction to the Singing of Psalm-Tunes *(1726). Reverend Tufts claimed that his little book would enable "children, or people of the meanest capacities" to learn to sight-read music.*

Moderately

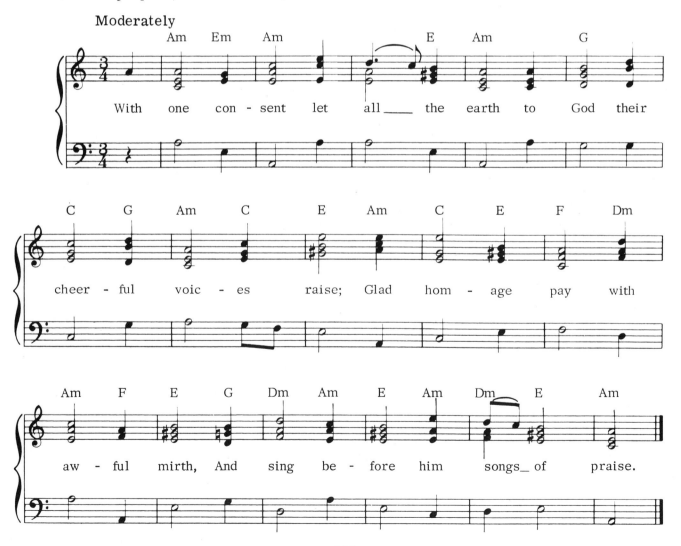

With one con - sent let all___ the earth to God their
cheer - ful voic - es raise; Glad hom - age pay with
aw - ful mirth, And sing be - fore him songs_ of praise.

Make a joyful noise unto the Lord, all ye lands.

2. Serve the Lord with gladness: come before his presence with singing.

3. Know ye that the Lord he is God: it is he that has made us, and not we ourselves; we are

GOD THE MASTER OF ALL PAGANS

In 1728 the Ephrata Cloister, a semimonastic religious community of Seventh-Day Baptists, was established in Pennsylvania by Johann Conrad Beissel (1690–1768). Immigrating from Germany at the age of 30, without any formal music education, Beissel not only founded and managed the cloister, but organized and trained a choir capable of sophisticated part-reading. He went on to compose over four hundred hymns for his choir, some with as many as eight parts. At Ephrata the music apparently was sung in a falsetto voice, with the mouth barely open, producing, we are told, a "soft measured cadence of sweet harmony."

"God the Master of All Pagans" is taken from Beissel's major hymn collection, Turtel-Taube, published in 1747. The text given here is a translation from the original German.

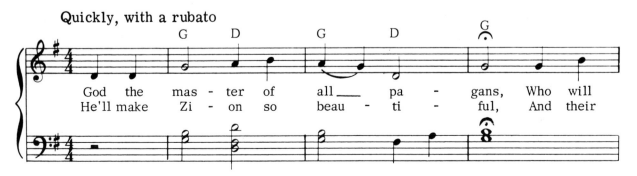

Quickly, with a rubato

God the mas - ter of all___ pa - gans, Who will
He'll make Zi - on so beau - ti - ful, And their

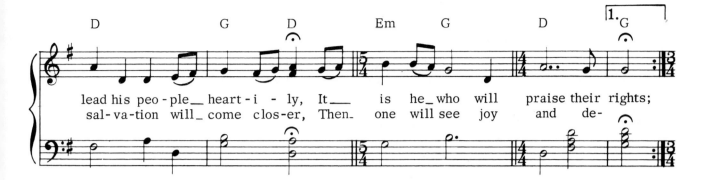

lead his peo-ple___ heart-i - ly, It___ is he_ who will praise their rights;
sal-va-tion will_ come clos-er, Then_ one will see joy and de-

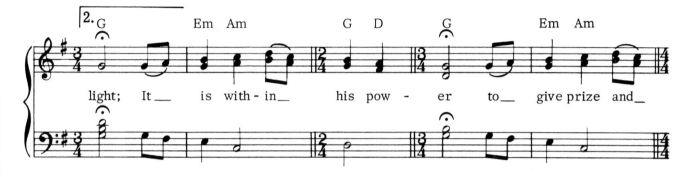

light; It ___ is with-in_ his pow - er to_ give prize and_

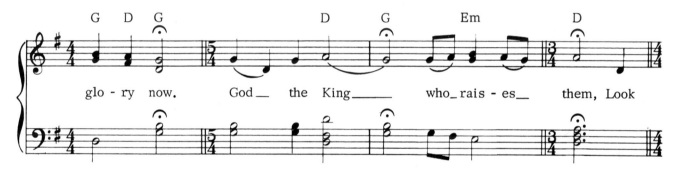

glo - ry now. God __ the King_____ who_ rais - es_ them, Look

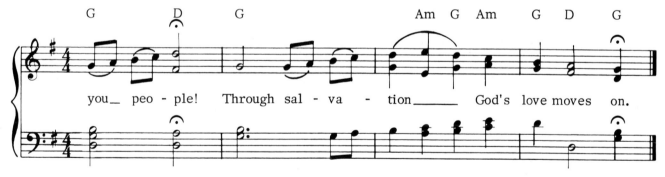

you_ peo - ple! Through sal - va - tion_____ God's love moves on.

135

WHEN JESUS WEPT

In the realm of "serious" music, William Billings (1746–1800) was America's first important composer. A self-educated musician, he began his career as an itinerant music teacher, going from church to church instructing various congregations in the art of singing. Though he sang in a loud and harsh voice, he had a contagious enthusiasm for music that kept him heavily in demand.

The following canon, set here to be sung as a round, was published in Billings's first collection, The New-England Psalm-Singer, *in 1770.*

This round is designed to be sung by four voices, although it can be executed successfully by as few as two. The round begins with one singer alone. As he moves to the second line, another singer begins the first line. As the first singer begins the third line, the second singer starts the second line and a third singer begins the first line. Four bars later a fourth voice enters with the first line. Each singer sings the complete round twice.

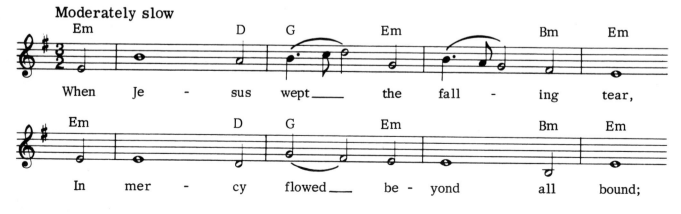

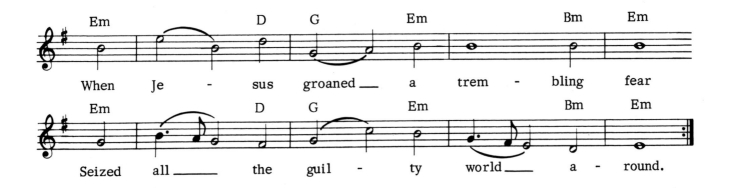

When Je - sus groaned a trem - bling fear

Seized all the guil - ty world a - round.

THUS SAITH THE HIGH,
THE LOFTY ONE

Here is Billings in a sturdy canon, an attractive example of his gift for melody. The text is from book one of Hymns and Spiritual Songs *(London, 1709), by Isaac Watts, the author of many hymns still sung in America today. The music was originally published in Billings's* The New-England Psalm-Singer. *Here Billings writes:*

> *It is well known that there is more variety in one piece of fuging music, than in twenty pieces of plain song, for while the tones do most sweetly coincide and agree, the words are seemingly engaged in a musical warfare. . . . Each part seems determined by dint of harmony and strength of accent, to drown his competitor in an ocean of harmony, and while each part is thus mutually striving for mastery, and sweetly contending for victory, the audience are most luxuriously entertained, and exceedingly delighted. . . . O enchanting! O ecstatic! Push on, push on ye sons of harmony!*

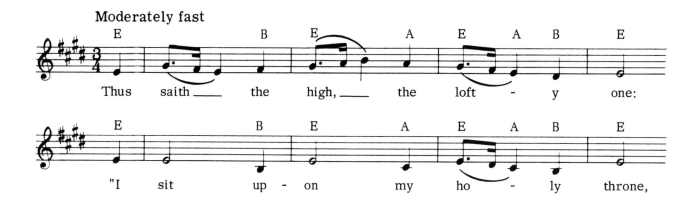

My name＿ is God, ＿ I dwell＿ on high;

Dwell in ＿ my own ＿ e - ter - ni - ty."

CHESTER

"Chester," one of William Billings's most popular compositions, was first published in 1778 in The Singing-Master's Assistant. *This book was one of six collections of tunes that Billings published for the use of singing schools. Because of its political references, the hymn was a great success and was soon adopted by everyone from churches to marching bands as the unofficial song of the Revolution.*

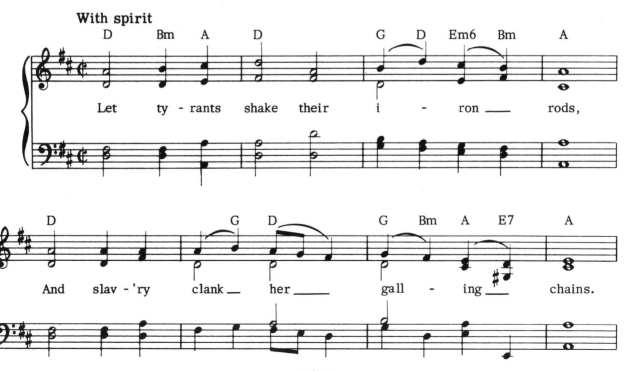

Let ty - rants shake their i - ron ___ rods,

And slav - 'ry clank ___ her ___ gall - ing ___ chains.

We fear them not, we — trust — in — God,

New — Eng-land's God —————— for - e - ver — reigns.

Howe and Burgoyne and Clinton,
    too,
With Prescott and Cornwallis joined,
Together plot our overthrow,
In one infernal league combined.

When God inspired us for the fight,
Their ranks were broke, their lines
    were forced,
Their ships were shattered in our
    sight,
Or swiftly driven from our coast.

The foe comes on with haughty
    stride,
Our troops advance with martial
    noise;
Their vet'rans flee before our youth,
And gen'rals yield to beardless boys.

What grateful off'ring shall we bring,
What shall we render to the Lord?
Loud hallelujahs let us sing,
And praise his name on ev'ry chord!

DAVID'S LAMENTATION

This setting of David's lament was composed by William Billings and published in The Singing-Master's Assistant *in 1778. The somber message of the biblical text, from II Samuel 18, is effectively communicated by the melodic and harmonic treatment. On the singing of his compositions Billings wrote: "Strive to sing in the spirit as well as with the understanding: and God grant we may so conduct ourselves here, as to be admitted into that land of Harmony, where we may in tuneful Hozannahs and eternal Hallelujahs, Shout the REDEEMER."*

went, he wept and said: "O, my son! O, my son!

Would to God I had died, Would to God I had died, Would to

God I had died for thee, O, Ab-sal-om, my son, my son."

JARGON

Certain people ridiculed the New England composer William Bill-ings. They complained that in his first tune book, The New-England Psalm-Singer *(1770), he used unorthodox harmonies and texts. "Jargon" is his answer to these critics. Published in his* The Singing-Master's Assistant *(1778), it consists almost entirely of dissonant chords, the opening one being the only exception. But it is nevertheless a masterpiece, since, as one writer has noted, the individual parts are easily singable.*

greet the ear, _____ As ter – ri – ble as thun-der!

ff

145

NEW-PLYMOUTH

Of his "New-Plymouth," William Billings wrote: "Suitable to be sung on the Anniversary of our Forefathers' landing in New England, Nov. 20th. Anno Domini 1620." As an afterthought, he added: "Rouse ye Yankees and celebrate this Anniversary, and do not say on the 21st day of November, 'I forgot what day it was yesterday.'"

The hymn, first published in Billings's The Continental Harmony *(1794), uses as text a metrical version of Psalm 44 from Tate and Brady's* New Version of the psalms *(1698).*

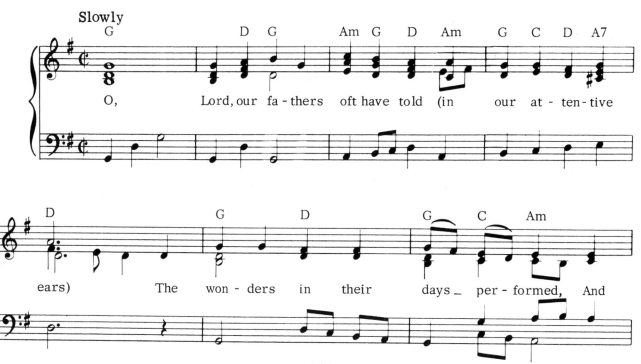

VICTORY

The text of this hymn by William Billings indicates that the composer may have intended it to be sung following an American triumph in the field—by soldiers and civilians alike. Originally published in The Continental Harmony *(1794)—Billings's last and most ambitious tune book—it is appropriately named "Victory." Billings attributed the words to Dr. Watts.*

found the foe,＿ and melt ＿ their strength a - way. 'Tis

by thine aid our＿ troops pre-vail, And＿ break u - nit -ed＿ pow'rs! Or

burn their boast-ed＿ fleets! Or＿ scale the＿ proud-est of＿ their＿ tow'rs!

HOLLAND

Like other New England singing masters of his day, Daniel Read (1757–1841) was a man of many talents: composer, Revolutionary soldier, manufacturer of combs, and founder of The American Musical Magazine, *the first music periodical in the United States. In addition, Read published several collections of tunes; his most successful was* The American Singing Book *(published in 1785), from which the song "Holland" is taken. In this book Read includes a set of instructions for keeping time while singing: "In order to give these notes and rests their proper time [in 4/4 meter], a motion of the hand is necessary. . . . This [meter] has four beats in each bar, which should be beat . . . in the following manner, VIZ. First, lightly strike the ends of your fingers, secondly, the heel of your hand, thirdly, raise your hand a little and shut it up, fourthly, raise it still higher and throw it open at the same time, which completes the bar." Read, like other music teachers, felt that such gestures were necessary to keep the rhythm constant and to combat the "common way", or rote tradition, of singing.*

"Holland" may have been meant to be sung at weddings. The words for the song—"for happy Matches"—are by Isaac Watts.

CHINA

"China," named after a town in Maine, was composed by Timothy Swan (1758–1842), noted American psalmodist and compiler of both sacred and secular songs. It was probably written in 1790 and first sung in public in 1794, although it did not appear in print until after 1800. With a text taken from Isaac Watts's Hymns and Spiritual Songs, Book II (London, 1709), "China" quickly became a popular hymn.

The tune is remarkably beautiful and unmistakably American. Sung at funerals in New England for over a hundred years, "China" can still be found in Southern hymnals today.

Why should we mourn de - part - ing friends, Or

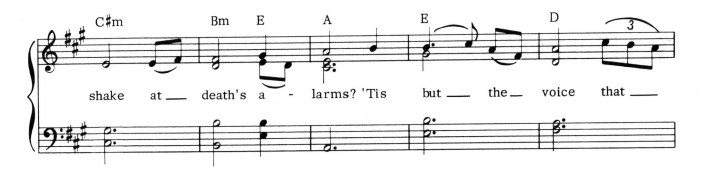

shake at ___ death's a - larms? 'Tis but ___ the ___ voice that ___

Je - sus ___ sends, To ___ call them ___ to his ___ arms.

AMERICA

This somber adaptation of the Twenty-third Psalm is accredited to
the American psalmodist Wetmore and is taken from a collection
entitled Social Harmony (1798), by Asahel Benham (1757–1805).
In a set of instructions preceding the songs, Benham writes: "The
perfection of singing is to pronounce the words, and make the
sounds as feelingly as if the sentiments and sounds were our own.
If singers, when performing a piece of music, could be as much capti-
vated with the words and sounds, as the Author of the music is when
composing it . . . they would pronounce, accent, swell, sing loud and
soft where the words require it; make suitable gestures, and add
every other necessary grace."

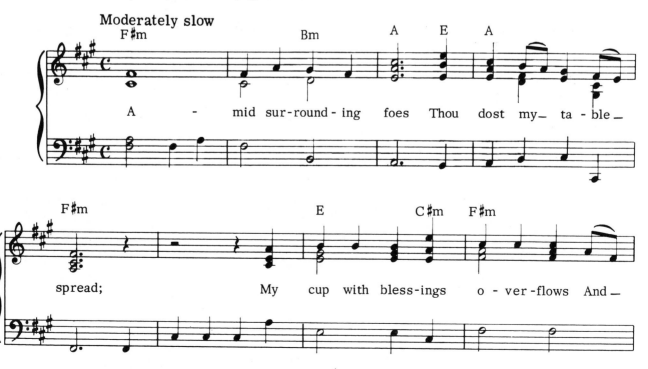

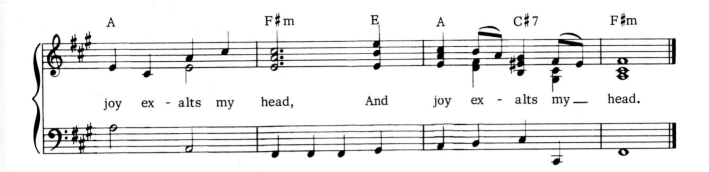

joy ex - alts my head, And joy ex - alts my __ head.

A FAVORITE
CHRISTMAS HYMN

When celebrating Christmas, the colonists turned to such songs as this, taken from Jonathan Huntington's Albany Collection *(1800). Born in Connecticut, Huntington (1771–1838) was a professional singer, song writer, and compiler of tune books. In the preface to the* Albany Collection *he notes: "Vocal Music is without doubt one of the most Pleasing and Useful sciences when rightly understood, and well performed, by reason of its being made use of to sound forth the praise and glory of the grand Parent of the universal world; who formed our bodies, and endowed us with a share of understanding, and formed in us an expressive voice, that we may sound his praise in this world below."*

OMEGA

"Omega" was written by Supply Belcher (1751–1836) and published in his tune book The Harmony of Maine *in 1794. Belcher earned the title of "the Handel of Maine" for his elaborate compositions. He was also noted for his charming tunes, such as this one, which although quite simple is surprisingly effective. The well-known text, first published about 1757, is sometimes sung to the tune of "God Save the King," the same melody used for "God Save the Thirteen States" earlier in this book. The author of the text is unknown.*

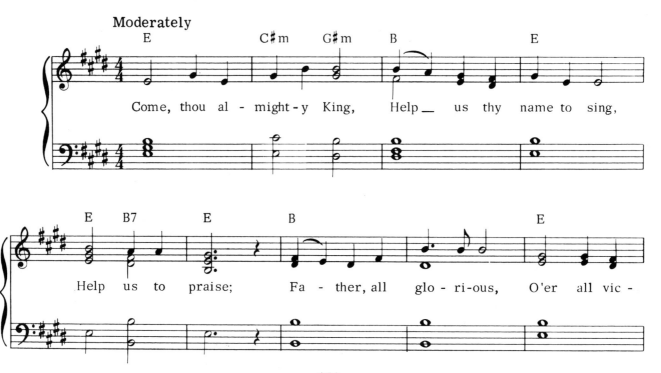